The Organization Whisperer

12 Core Actions

that Ripple Excellence through Your Organization

INSIDE: Download your **FREE**
Organization Whisperer Toolkit

David Childs, PhD

*The Organization Whisperer: 12 Core Actions
that Ripple Excellence through Your Organization*

ISBN 978-0-9971094-0-5 Print
ISBN 978-0-9971094-1-2 E-Book

Author's Note: We have attempted to identify ownership of all cartoon illustrations and quotes used. In some cases we have been unsuccessful in identifying original creator or source. Should any of these belong to you, please contact me through my website and we will provide proper attribution.

Printed in the United States of America

AUTHOR WEBSITE
www.TheOrganizationWhisperer.com

Table of Contents

What Is an Organization Whisperer?

The Organization Whisperer Leadership Diagnostic

The Twelve Core Actions

Core Action #1 — Communication

Core Action #2 — Worth

Core Action #3 — Purpose

Core Action #4 — Family

Core Action #5 — Decisions

Core Acton #6 — Plan

Core Action #7 — Do

Core Action #8 — Measure

Core Action #9 — Processes

Core Action #10 — Resources

Core Action #11 — Relationships

Core Action #12 — Habit

Final Thoughts

What Is an Organization Whisperer?

FABLE: A Wise Owl took his students to the shore of a beautiful lake. He tossed a small rock high into the sky, and they watched it drop into the water. The students watched the ripples that the small rock had created spread out, influencing a wide area of the lake's placid surface. "Many people prefer the calm sameness and stillness of the lake surface as we first found it," the Wise Owl said. "Other people like to create ripples or even waves on the water. But the wise person is fascinated by the search for the original core action, in this case the tossing of the rock, that created the ripples. The universe is comprised of many core actions—gravity, the speed of light, and love. Every discipline, from engineering to medical care, from music to leadership, has core actions. The rewarding intellectual life is nourished by the search for and understanding of these core actions."

REAL LIFE: After Vince Lombardi and his Green Bay Packers won the first two Super Bowls, a standing-room-only crowd of coaches packed a ballroom to hear the legend share his wisdom. A promising young college coach was given the honor of introducing Lombardi. Seizing the opportunity to promote himself before such a large audience, the young coach launched into a forty-minute promotion of his own offense's plays, schemes, audibles, and brilliant complexities.

When he finally gave up the microphone, Lombardi approached and said, "Many of you have been standing for a long time, so I will be brief. The Green Bay Packers only run twelve plays, but we think they are twelve pretty effective plays."

THIS BOOK STANDS APART from most organizational management and leadership books. While most books on leadership basically agree on the theoretical secrets of effective organizational leaders and **WHAT** successful leaders do, very few books help you identify **WHERE** your organization rates today or reveal the specific **HOWs** that will convert the theory of success into reality. None of those books offer the twelve winning plays sure to create ripples of excellence and success in your organization.

The Organization Whisperer equips you with a complete set of tools that help you assess where your organization is currently on the continuum of excellence and provides the core actions that will help you improve performance. These twelve plays are proven to move your organization from its current state to excellence. This is a working book that provides a direct, practical approach to organizational improvement.

As an example, many books will advise you to "hire quality people." This book will tell you **HOW** to identify whether a particular job applicant possesses the desired core quality character traits by providing you with an *Interview Grade Sheet* that focuses on the desired traits. It will also provide key interview questions proven to be effective at helping your organization determine whether the applicant possesses the desired qualities. This single tool can lead to dramatic results for your organization.

Other books advise you to "create an innovative culture." This book will show you **HOW** to create such a culture by providing you with simple, fast, and specific actions that will unleash the innovative culture that already exists within your organization. Organizations that adopt the core practices revealed in this book realize astounding results. During the course of a single year, one organization identified seventy-five recommendations for improvements. Within that same year, the organization implemented fifty-three of those recommendations.

In addition to providing twelve core actions for excellence, this book also contains *The Organization Whisperer Leadership Diagnostic* to help you determine **WHERE** your organization currently is on the continuum from average to excellent, and each chapter contains a brief Litmus Test that will tell you where your organization currently is along the continuum moving toward excellence as it relates to the specific core action discussed in that chapter.

Secrets of the Organization Whisperer

What is an organization whisperer? An organization whisperer is a leader who has mastered the art of assessing where the organization is and responding to its current state with focused, specific actions that develop organizational excellence. Just as dog and horse whisperers have learned the core essences of dogs and horses, organization whisperers have learned how to quickly assess organizational priorities, procedures, and culture to determine where an organization currently is on the scale of average to excellent. Furthermore, an organization whisperer knows the core actions needed to ripple the organization toward excellence.

The core actions we will explore in this book require very little implementation time, yet they have consistently produced improvements of from twenty to forty percent in the first year, an additional ten percent in the second year, and an ongoing sustainable performance improvement level of five percent each year. This impact has been consistently achieved across multiple organizational cultures, and these actions will produce the same results in your organization.

Adopt a Symbol of Excellence

A powerful way to crystallize a concept is to create an image that can serve as a philosophical compass. Mickey Mouse superbly symbolizes the mission of the Disney organization. A small, inexpensive, but satisfying, package of nuts brilliantly symbolizes Southwest Airlines' mission and culture. Adopting a symbol or image of your desired organizational culture provides a simple visual image as well as a go-to benchmark for evaluating leadership on a day-to-day basis.

One way to create an excellent clear mental image of the difference between mediocre and excellent organizations is to reflect on the differences between two imaginary pigs. These two pigs led two different farms by very different leadership philosophies and, consequently, produced very different results. One pig, Napoleon, dictated and "top-downed" Animal Farm into poverty and rebellion, while a second pig named Babe, who lived on a neighboring farm, proved to be a natural organization whisperer who "bottom upped" Hoggett Farm to cooperative teamwork and success.

Babe's leadership style and his results, compared to Napoleon's, provide a clear model for organization whisperer leadership. After every meeting, conversation, or decision-making process, ask yourself, "Am I modeling Napoleon or Babe? Am I turning my organization into Animal Farm or Hoggett Farm?" As you evaluate your day-to-day decisions and leadership actions by constantly asking yourself if you are modeling Babe or Napoleon (or your own chosen symbol of excellence), you will begin to naturally model, live, and become an organization whisperer.

Notes to the Reader

You are not expected to implement every core action recommended in this book at once. Obviously, the more actions that you do take, the more ripples that you will create and the more dramatically your organization will improve. Some organizations may already be excellent in some categories but not in others. You may wish to take a few actions at first, then add more as you progress.

The twelve core actions are intentionally designed to either complement each other or to stand on their own. Implementing these core actions is guaranteed to improve your organization, regardless of how you choose to implement them. Simply begin and notice the changes within your organization.

If you need clarification, counsel, or advice while either reading this book or implementing its recommendations, feel free to contact me at: fitforservice@verizon.net. I would be honored to be of assistance to you and your organization. Please also let me know how implementing these recommendations has benefitted your organization. It is always a joy to hear success stories, and sharing your specific results could benefit other organization whisperers.

The Organization Whisperer Leadership Diagnostic

LET'S START THE JOURNEY TOWARD EXCELLENCE. First, let's find out where your organization is today so that, as it improves, you can document and appreciate that improvement. We will begin with a *Leadership Diagnostic* to clarify where your organization currently is on the journey from average to excellent.

Know that initially you may not score very well. This journey is not about where you are today. Rather, it is about all of the improvements that you are going to make and be able to document and celebrate. This is about how much higher you are going to score next time and the time after that as you implement the core actions recommended in this book.

If you wish, ask other managers and staff within your organization to take the diagnostic test as well. It might even be fun for a group of you to complete the test and discuss it together. This consensus-building conversation will lay the foundations to get everyone on the same page and prepared to move your organization toward excellence. As you document where you are today and learn the actions that need to be taken to get you where you want to go, you equip the team to work together toward rippling the organization forward.

The diagnostic begins on the next page. Enjoy!

The Organization Whisperer Toolkit
The Organization Whisperer Leadership Diagnostic

This leadership diagnostic cites core actions of excellent organizations and helps you determine how many of these core actions are already being practiced in your organization. Complete the diagnostic here or download your free *Organization Whisperer Toolkit* online at www.theorganizationwhisperer.com/kit.

Date: _____ Organization: _____ Position: Top / Middle / Front-Line

MISSION	
How do you rate your organization in the following best practices?	
BEST PRACTICE	**Rank from Lousy to Outstanding** 1__2__3__4__5__6__7__8__9__10
1. **BRIEF:** Board, staff easily recite the mission statement from heart.	
2. **FOCUSED:** The mission focuses and directs organizational behavior.	
3. **ALIGNED:** Employees can explain how their job contributes to achieving the mission.	
4. **UNIQUE:** The mission honors the organization's unique purpose.	
5. **VISIONARY:** The mission provides a sense of purpose, worth, and value.	
TOTAL POINTS 5-15 Minimal 16-30 Somewhat 31-40 Advanced 41-50 Excellent	**SCORE**

EMPOWERMENT

How do you rate your organization in the following best practices?

BEST PRACTICE	Rank from Lousy to Outstanding 1__2__3__4__5__6__7__8__9__10
1. This organization places a high priority on recruiting positive "Can Do" and empathetic "Service Focused" personalities.	
2. The interview and selection process includes participation by key staff from departments that will work directly with the person if hired.	
3. New employees are thoroughly oriented and trained in the organization's culture, mission, and processes.	
4. Professional development and personal growth are important goals of the employee performance review process.	
5. Employee raises and promotions are based on positive attitudes, motivated commitment to the mission, and excellent performance.	
6. Organizational communication is open, honest, constructive, and mission-focused.	
TOTAL POINTS 6-18 Minimal 19-36 Somewhat 37-48 Advanced 49-60 Excellent	**SCORE**

COUNT

How do you rate your organization in the following best practices?

BEST PRACTICE	Rank from Lousy to Outstanding 1__2__3__4__5__6__7__8__9__10
1. The organization measures performance outcomes.	
2. Performance measures are linked to the mission and strategic goals.	
3. Performance language (outputs, outcomes) is part of the organizational culture.	
4. Employees participate in quality/performance measurement training.	
5. Employees are empowered and encouraged to contribute to organizational goals, objectives and performance monitoring.	
6. Performance measurement knowledge, experience and results are a high priority in supervisory positions and a crucial part of hiring criteria.	
7. Programs, services, departments and core processes all have specific performance goals that are understood and monitored.	
8. Performance measures for quality customer service and satisfaction are collected, monitored, reported and improved.	
9. Comparative measures are collected and reported (trends, competition, peer agencies, process and program benchmarks, etc.).	
10. The organization collects a variety of performance measures and maintains a live monitoring of the most critical.	
11. Performance reports are easily and quickly produced; and are user friendly.	
12. Performance data is audited for accuracy and reliability.	
13. Performance data is transparent and reported monthly/quarterly.	

14. Performance measures drive personnel evaluations and compensation.	
15. Constant measurable improvement is a core value of the organization.	
16. Performance measurement data is used to make and support decisions.	
17. Supervisors and employees are trained to read and analyze reports, and to constructively adapt so as to better achieve desired outcomes.	
18. Performance evaluation and improvement workshops are conducted twice a year.	
19. Employees at all levels participate in performance evaluation and in improvement workshops.	
20. High-performing departments, teams and employees are recognized and acknowledged for their work.	
TOTAL POINTS 20-60 Minimal 61-120 Somewhat 121-160 Advanced 161-200 Excellent	**SCORE**

ADAPT

How do you rate your organization in the following best practices?

BEST PRACTICE	Rank from Lousy to Outstanding 1__2__3__4__5__6__7__8__9__10
1. A strategic planning retreat of the full board and key staff is held annually.	
2. Employees are empowered to participate in the strategic planning process and are involved in implementation.	
3. 75% or more of strategic plan objectives are successfully implemented within two years.	
4. More time, staff, and resources are invested in pursuing pro-active improvements than in re-acting to unanticipated challenges.	
5. Strategic planning and prioritizing of implementation are driven by how to better achieve the mission.	
6. Strategic implementations and their measureable impacts are tracked and transparently reported monthly or quarterly.	
7. Creativity, experimentation, and learning from failures are encouraged, recognized, and rewarded.	
TOTAL POINTS 7-21 Minimal 22-42 Somewhat 43-56 Advanced 57-70 Excellent	**SCORE**

TOTAL SCORES

How do you rate your organization in the following best practices?

FOCUS AREA	TOTAL POINTS				SCORE
Mission	5-15 Minimal	16-30 Somewhat	31-40 Advanced	41-50 Excellent	
Empowerment	6-18 Minimal	19-36 Somewhat	37-48 Advanced	49-60 Excellent	
Count	20-60 Minimal	61-120 Somewhat	121-160 Advanced	161-200 Excellent	
Adapt	7-21 Minimal	22-42 Somewhat	43-56 Advanced	57-70 Excellent	

TOTAL POINTS | | | | | **SCORE**
38-114 Minimal   115-228 Somewhat   229-304 Advanced   305-380 Excellent

Core Action #1—Communication

Moving from Negative, Me-Focused
to Positive, Team-Focused

In any organization, there is a direct relationship between the
number of employee smiles and the percentage of profit margins.

ALLEGORY: A man is driving on a narrow and curvy high alpine road that had no railings and a sheer drop on one side. Suddenly, another car comes swerving toward him from around a bend. He veers toward the mountainside rather than the cliff side of the road. As the other car careens past him, only inches away, the driver yells, *"Pig!"* Incensed and outraged that this idiot not only almost killed both of them but also had the ignorant audacity to blame the incident on him, the man yells back over his shoulder, *"Hog!"* He then drives around the bend and crashes into the pig.

REAL LIFE: A new CEO could not get his inherited second V.P. to perform such assigned duties as reading and producing reports or conducting cost-benefit analyses. Instead of attending to these duties, the V.P. spent his days performing physical tasks such as repairing equipment, changing light bulbs, and supervising moves. In order to gain more insight into this man so he might learn how to best guide him toward the more mentally challenging and sophisticated duties that the CEO wanted the V.P. to fulfill, the CEO began "shooting the breeze" with his V.P. over morning coffee.

Sure enough, after about three weeks of seemingly casual conversation, the sixty-year old V.P. related that when he was in the third grade he was a poor reader and speller. As a result, he never participated in the weekly spelling bees. But one Friday when the teacher called out a word he felt confident he knew how to spell, he excitedly thrust his hand up so that he could be given the opportunity to excel.

The V.P. then quoted to the CEO the exact words that the teacher had said to him fifty-two years earlier. "So, Johnny, you think you know one?" So it was that, for the next fifty-two years, those seven words had influenced this man to avoid reading, writing, and any other tasks requiring intellectual knowledge or mental prowess.

WHAT Excellent Organizations Do Differently

The core, foundational difference between excellent and mediocre organizations is that excellent organizations create a culture in which communication is positive, constructive, and mission-focused. In mediocre organizations, communication is much more negative in tone and self-focused. One can very easily, quickly, and accurately determine the quality of an organization by simply listening to "the tone" of conversation in the break room. Period.

Specifically, excellent organizations monitor and constantly improve their communications in four targeted areas. Let's examine these one by one.

Internal Communication

All internal communications are positive, constructive, and focused on organizational improvement.

External Communication

REAL LIFE: An organization posted a "You Will Need..." checklist in order to inform their customers which documents would be needed in order to successfully complete their business. Good idea. Unfortunately, the sign was posted not where customers would see it as they were entering the organization, but on the "Exit" door. This meant that customers still came in unprepared, unaware, and uninformed. They still waited in line only to be turned away, because a well-intended sign was placed in an ineffective location.

REAL LIFE: An organization added a "5 Most Requested Services" page to their website. The page provided those services in a simple, user-friendly manner. Use of the website tripled, and demand for in-person and telephone services dropped significantly.

External communications with customers, partners, and vendors should be equally positive, constructive, and mutually beneficial.

High-Tech, High-Touch

Excellent organizations make a priority of investing in fast, smart, sophisticated technology that excellently performs routine, repetitive, back-room, and / or grunt tasks so that personnel are freed up to prioritize quality, personal customer service.

FABLE: Two Little Pigs decided to build a house of lumber. The house site was five miles from the nearest lumber yard. One piggy walked to the lumber yard, because this little piggy had no truck. He said, "I need lumber." The lumber man asked, "What size of lumber do you need?" and offered his cell phone so the piggy could discuss it with the other piggy. But, alas, the other piggy did not have a cell phone, so the piggy walked the ten mile round trip and reported back to the lumber man: "2 x 4's."

The lumber man replied, "That's good, but how many?" The lumber man offered his laptop computer so that the piggy could e-mail the other piggy, but, alas, the piggies did not have a computer either. The piggy returned from his ten-mile trip again and reported to the lumber man: "I'll take four hundred 2x4's." Then the lumber man offered to load his own truck with the lumber and let the piggy drive it to the work site. But, alas, only the piggy at the work site knew how to drive; so, the piggy set off to send the other piggy back to drive the truck.

Unfortunately, on his way, a wolf ate him.

360 Chinese Listening

The symbol for "listening" in the written Chinese language includes not only the symbol for "ears," but also the symbol for "eyes" and the symbol for "heart." This underscores the fact that true listening is not half-hearing with one ear while also doing something else. Rather, true, intense listening includes observing facial expressions and body language, and empathizing with the emotions that are being expressed. Chinese listening is a priority. It is a full-contact sport, and excellent organizations practice it.

360 Listening means that the entire organization, from janitor to CEO, practice "Chinese Listening" with everyone else. Everyone is in it together, on equal footing, working together constructively to achieve the organization's mission. All excellent organizations practice Chinese 360 listening.

WHY Excellent Organizations Do It Differently

Excellent organizations know that the core action of cultivating a positive staff creates the ripples of: 1) happy customers, 2) increased staff retention, experience, and wisdom, 3) commitment and loyalty to the organization along with increased voluntary productivity, and, finally, 4) increased organizational innovation. (Positive, happy working environments encourage creative thinking. Put another way, hah-hah promotes ah-hah.)

The documented verification of these points was provided in a recent exhaustive study by Gallup. The study analyzed 2.5 million managers and 27 million employees in organizations across 195 countries and found that organizations that had created and sustained progressive, constructive, positive cultures experienced the following specific "success ripples":

- 19 percent improved staff stability
- 22.5 percent improved productivity
- 48 percent improved profitability
- 5 to 7 percent sustained annual improvement

The same study also found that 82 percent of hires into management positions were based upon resume-listed skills, seniority, or personal relationships, while only 18 percent of hires into management-level positions were based upon an applicant's demonstrated ability to create and sustain a progressive, constructive organizational culture, the key foundational cornerstone to building an excellent organization that achieves the four "success ripples" documented above.

WHERE Is Your Organization Today?

Litmus Test #1 will provide insight regarding where your organization currently is on the journey along the continuum from having organizational communication that is negative in tone and me-focused to organizational communication that is positive and team-focused.

LITMUS TEST #1: Communication

Complete here or download your free *Organization Whisperer Toolkit* online at www.theorganizationwhisperer.com/kit.

⊙ Take the "Communications Litmus Test" at the end of this chapter.

⊙ Think of your organization's last three hires into management-level positions. For what specific reasons were the chosen applicants selected (resume skills, seniority, relationships, positive culture-building skills, other)? List the reasons below.

Hire #1 _____

Hire #2 _____

Hire #3 _____

⊙ Who are the three to five staff members who are the organization's most positive cheerleaders — not kiss-ups, but sincerely and positively invested in and committed to the organization? (Note: In truly excellent organizations, fully fifty percent of total staff could qualify for this category.) List names here:

1. _____

2. _____

3. _____

4. _____

5. _____

HOW to Become Excellent

Core Action #1 will provide you with specific actions that will ripple your organization's communications from being negative and "me" focused to being positive and team focused.

CORE ACTION #1

Internal Communication

Prioritize having a positive tone of communication throughout your organization.

- ✓ Personally (meaning you, the Organization Whisperer!) model constructive, positive communication... all day, every day.

- ✓ Smile. A lot.

- ✓ Be positive, professional, and developmental with every staff member in as personalized a manner as possible.

- ✓ Constantly display an attitude of expectation that, "Together we are making tomorrow better."

- ✓ Politely, progressively, consistently encourage positive communication among all staff at all levels of the organization — that begins when YOU set the example by modeling the expected attitudes and behaviors.

- ✓ Increase the involvement of "organizational cheerleaders" in key committees, meetings, and projects, so that these individuals can help you model desired constructive, positive attitudes, and behaviors.

- ✓ When challenged by the negative defeatists regarding the organizational insistence on a positive, constructive environment, respond that it is "good, smart business." You may choose to cite the four successful impact data bullets provided in the WHY section of this chapter and post the *Why Improve Today* poster found at the end of this chapter on the walls of your office and the conference rooms.

External Communication

Ensure that external communication with customers, partners, and vendors is equally positive and constructive. Begin by "walking a mile in the shoes" of your customers, business partners, and product vendors.

✓ Experience "the tone" of the various elements of your organization's communication systems. Are the communications positive, user-friendly, and provide correct information? Evaluate the following types of communication and record your observations.

- In-person (positive, user-friendly, correct):

- Telephone (recorded messages / menu / live) (positive, user-friendly, correct):

- E-mail (positive, user-friendly, correct):

- Website (positive, user-friendly, correct):

- Office Signage (positive, user-friendly, correct):

- Written Correspondence (positive, user-friendly, correct):

- Forms (positive, user-friendly, correct):

✓ Identify the five questions most commonly asked by customers and look for the answers on your organization's website. Could you easily find these answers?

✓   If you looked on the website for how to get in touch with a real person, is that information readily provided?

✓   If you send an e-mail to the organization, is there a response? How long did it take to receive a response?

✓   If you call into the telephone system and ask one of the top five commonly asked questions, do you get a correct and helpful answer?

✓   Are the various types of communication methods identified above user-friendly?

✓   Are they a positive experience?

✓   Based upon having "experienced the tone" of your organization's external communication services, list five key improvements that would make your external communications even more positive, informative, and user-friendly:

1. _____

2. _____

3. _____

4. _____

5. _____

High-Tech, High-Touch

Priority action items for rippling toward a more "high tech-high touch" organization are:

✓   Identify, with input from organizational staff, three routine, repetitive, and/or procedural tasks that technology could accomplish just as or more effectively than staff.

     1. _____

     2. _____

     3. _____

✓   Begin developing and implementing these specific technological applications in your organization.

360 Listening

Here are some ways to incorporate 360 Chinese Listening into your organization:

• Prioritize monthly meetings of the management team.

     ✓   Managers Meeting Date / Time: _____

• Prioritize monthly meetings of staff representatives who are chosen by the staff.

     ✓   Staff Representatives Meeting Date / Time: _____

• Identify specific meeting dates and times. For example: "We will meet on every second Monday at 10:00 a.m." Choose times that are most convenient to the schedules of the attendees. Decide on meeting times in your organization now:

- These meetings have one focus: to provide managers and staff the opportunity to express their recommendations for how to improve the organization. The tone of discussion will be about how to positively, constructively move the organization forward. Any discussion of unrelated topics or comments that negatively complain about perceived weaknesses will be redirected toward positive recommendations.

- At these meetings, senior management say little, other than to keep discussion properly focused. Top management's job is to:

  ✓ Chinese Listen 360!

  ✓ Take notes regarding the innovative recommendations that are presented, using the *Organization Improvement Projects Status* at the end of the chapter as an outline. Solicit volunteers from among gathered managers and staff who will "sponsor" a project and, with your support, pursue implementation.

  ✓ Between monthly meetings, discuss the progress status of current projects with these sponsors.

  ✓ At ensuing monthly meetings:

    - Discuss the progress status of current projects.
    - Celebrate completed projects.
    - Recognize their successful project sponsors.
    - Appreciate the improvements that the implemented project has brought to the organization.
    - Solicit innovative recommendations for more improvements.

WHO Will Perform This Action

You and your team of organizational cheerleaders will internally model and promote positive, constructive communication and 360 Chinese Listening in the monthly meetings, other organizational meetings and throughout your daily responsibilities. You, the cheerleaders, and additional staff who have subject-matter investments in particular areas identified for improvement, can implement the actions that have been recommended in the "External Communications" and the "High Tech / High Touch" sections.

Team Cheerleaders in Your Organization:

1. _____
2. _____
3. _____
4. _____
5. _____

External and High-Tech, High-Touch Projects and Subject-matter Invested Staff:

Project   *Invested Staff*

1. _____   _____
2. _____   _____
3. _____   _____
4. _____   _____
5. _____   _____

WHEN Will This Action Be Completed?

Obviously, sustaining a culture of positive communication is an ongoing process. However, the initial creation of a culture of positive communication should start as you are reading this book. As already stated, the culture of positive communication is the most critical cornerstone for your organization's success, and the remaining recommended actions in this book will produce exponentially greater impacts and benefits if they are implemented in an atmosphere of positive communication.

Begin today by demanding of yourself that you constantly model a positive, progressive demeanor in your role as an organization whisperer. Remember that any expressions of negativity can have lasting negative impacts on the staff and the organization. Remember that seven negative words in his childhood impacted the V.P.'s perspective and behavior for fifty-two years.

Identify your team of cheerleaders today. Announce the dates when you will begin your manager and staff meetings. Remember also that positive communication is the foundational difference between Napoleon's Animal Farm and Babe's Hoggett Farm. More positive organizations become more successful organizations.

The Organization Whisperer Toolkit
Communications Litmus Test

This leadership diagnostic will help you fine-tune organizational communication. To what degree is your organization currently exhibiting the following traits of quality communication? Complete here or download your free *Organization Whisperer Toolkit* at www.theorganizationwhisperer.com/kit.

Quality Characteristics of Empowered Communication

360 Listening
Circle one: {Lousy} 1 2 3 4 5 6 7 8 9 10 {Outstanding}

People Development
Circle one: {Lousy} 1 2 3 4 5 6 7 8 9 10 {Outstanding}

Empowers People
Circle one: {Lousy} 1 2 3 4 5 6 7 8 9 10 {Outstanding}

Mission Focused
Circle one: {Lousy} 1 2 3 4 5 6 7 8 9 10 {Outstanding}

Integrity and Trust
Circle one: {Lousy} 1 2 3 4 5 6 7 8 9 10 {Outstanding}

Positive Culture
Circle one: {Lousy} 1 2 3 4 5 6 7 8 9 10 {Outstanding}

Constant and Timely
Circle one: {Lousy} 1 2 3 4 5 6 7 8 9 10 {Outstanding}

The Organization Whisperer Toolkit
Why Improve Today

5%   19%   48%   22.5%

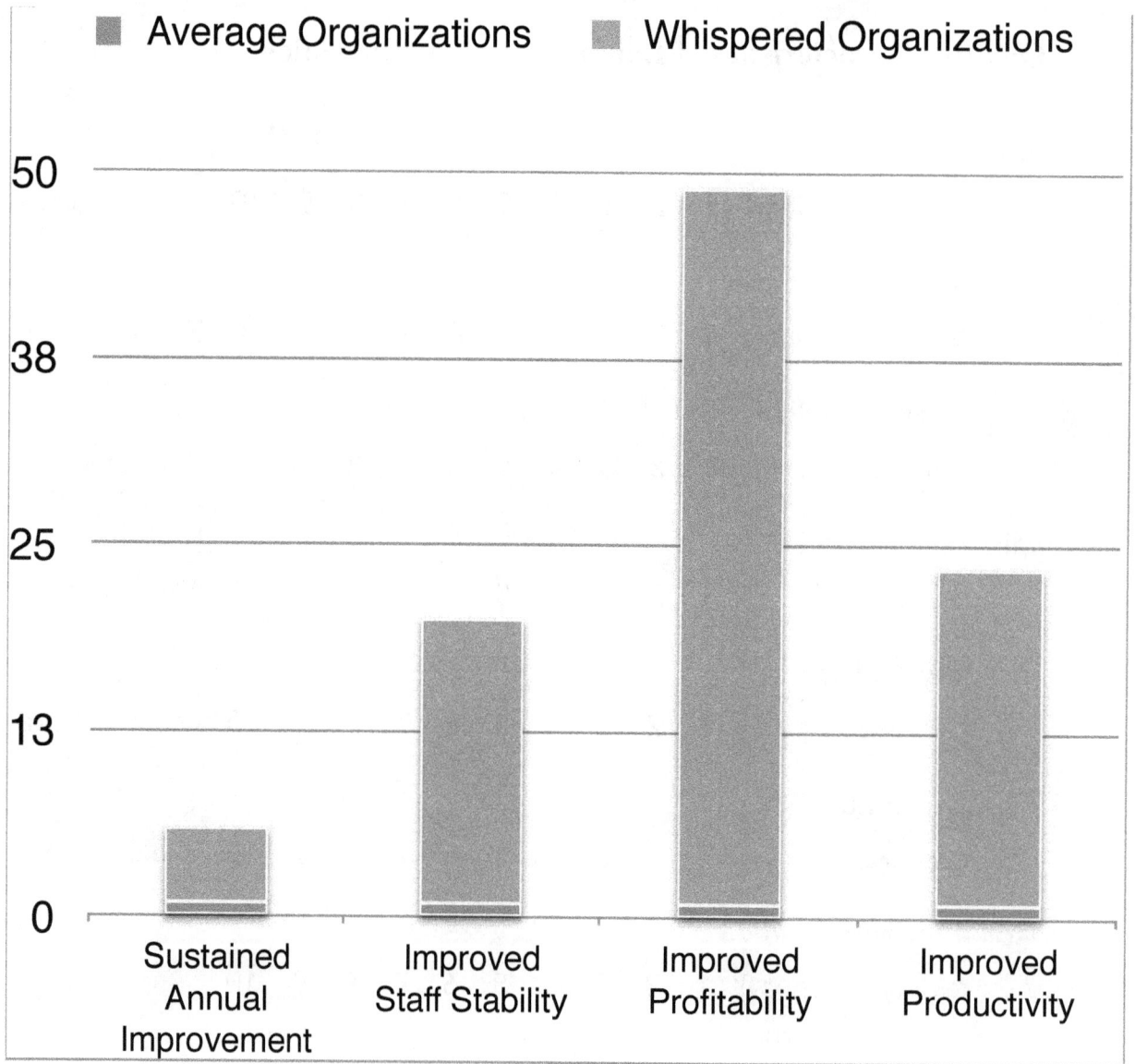

■ Average Organizations   ■ Whispered Organizations

	Sustained Annual Improvement	Improved Staff Stability	Improved Profitability	Improved Productivity

(Y-axis values: 0, 13, 25, 38, 50)

The Organization Whisperer Toolkit
Organization Improvement Projects Status

The *Organization Improvement Projects Status* tool will help you take notes regarding the progress status of current projects as well as document new improvements that have been proposed during the manager and the staff meetings. Complete here or download your free *Organization Whisperer Toolkit* from our website here: www.theorganizationwhisperer.com/kit.

PROJECT PRIORITY	PROJECT DESCRIPTION	STATUS	SPONSOR

Core Action—#2 Worth

Moving from Doing a Job to Making a Contribution

*Lousy managers make today worse. Average managers
survive today. Leaders make tomorrow better.*

*The art of leadership accomplishes
what the science of management says can't be done.*

REAL LIFE: A video by the charitable organization Heifer Project chronicles the impact of providing some dairy cows to an impoverished family in the Appalachians. The farm owner describes how the milk produced by the cows helped to improve his own family's nutrition while also providing surplus milk and butter that could be sold for additional income. Then the farmer cited an unexpected, but equally important, impact.

He told of how his mentally challenged brother used to be reserved and kept to himself. But once the brother was taught how to feed, brush, and care for the cows, he had come completely out of his shell, had been totally immersed into the family, and couldn't wait to get up every morning and get to the barn. With tears in his eyes, the farmer said, "All this time, my brother just needed to feel like he could contribute."

WHAT Excellent Organizations Do Differently

Excellent organizations place a high priority on making every employee feel like they are a valued contributor to an important mission. Employees are given tasks that the employee is most skilled at and most desires to do, and the employees are constantly reminded of how important to the whole organization their task is, even if it is nothing more than being the "official coffee maker." Every employee who is worth hiring wants to feel that they are making an important contribution to an important mission. Excellent organizations provide that opportunity.

WHY Excellent Organizations Do It Differently

Excellent organizations create an atmosphere of both human and organizational worth because it works. One very successful investment company makes their investments on the basis of "an organization's culture" rather than on financial and marketing projections. Over a recent ten-year period the companies that this firm invested in showed stock gains of 17.8 percent while the Standard and Poor average for that period was 2.8 percent.

Likewise, a recent study of companies that had earned the prestigious Malcolm Baldrige Quality Award, based upon creating positive performance management cultures, found that those companies showed sustained profit-growth margins that were double the national average. Companies that implement Baldrige and lean management principles into their organizational cultures consistently achieve performance effectiveness and efficiency levels that are 25 to 40 percent superior to that of companies that lack such cultures.

WHERE Is Your Organization Today?

Litmus Test #2 will help you determine where your organization is today on the journey toward having an organizational culture that creates an atmosphere of worth.

LITMUS TEST #2: Worth

Complete here or download the *Organization Whisperer Toolkit:* www.theorganizationwhisperer.com/kit.

⦿ Identify three challenges that your organization currently faces:

1. _____

2. _____

3. _____

⦿ Describe the actions that have been taken during the last six months to respond to these challenges:

1. _____

2. _____

3. _____

⦿ What do your measures and data indicate regarding how successfully your organization has responded to these challenges during the past six months:

1. _____

2. _____

3. _____

⦿ Describe the next actions that should be taken to improve in these three areas:

1. _____

2. _____

3. _____

Excellent organizations ask and answer these questions each and every day. It is what they do and who they are. Constantly asking and answering these questions contributes to the overall organizational atmosphere that everyone in the organization is constantly contributing toward organizational improvement, and thereby having a sense of value and worth to the organization.

HOW to Become Excellent

Core Action #2 will help your organization take specific actions that will ripple your organization toward a stronger atmosphere of worth.

CORE ACTION #2

✓ Tomorrow morning, disperse the Litmus Test #2 questions (above) to all team members of your organization, from the CEO to the janitor. Tell them that the organization is prioritizing some improvement projects and that you would appreciate their recommendations regarding how to improve the organization. Ask that their responses be returned to you by lunch.

✓ Then, in the afternoon, summarize the responses and issue the summarized responses to all staff, thanking them for their contributions to this project and telling them to expect additional requests for their recommendations to organizational improvement efforts in the near future.

WHO Will Perform This Action

You and any associates or assistants who you believe would enjoy working with you on the rest of this journey through the twelve actions presented in this book. The experience gained through the process of implementing these actions can be very beneficial to staff members who you are considering to bring into your organization's leadership succession planning. Get them involved now, on the ground floor.

You currently consider your potential Succession Leadership Team to include:

1. _____

2. _____

3. _____

4. _____

5. _____

WHEN Will This Action Be Completed?

By close of business tomorrow. Excellent organizations know that excellent performance is fleeting and elusive, and that to occasionally succeed at achieving it requires constant, focused urgency. Make creating worth a priority. Begin by addressing opportunities for improvement revealed in the answers to the questions that comprise Litmus Test #2 above.

Core Action #3—Purpose

Moving from Aimless to Goal-Directed

*If you don't know where you are going,
then you are pretty certain not to get there.*

*The chances of achieving a goal are improved
if we are inspired by the nobility of the goal.*

REAL LIFE: Burning Rubber Tire Company had been sued several times for poor quality of work. Flats that had supposedly been fixed went flat again. Even worse, new tires that had not been adequately installed had come off of the cars while they were being driven, causing several serious accidents. The tire company asked an organization whisperer to advise them regarding how to reduce the expensive lawsuits.

The consultant's advice was that every mechanic should place in their work bay a picture of their loved ones. The reason for doing this was to remind the mechanics that their job, their purpose, their mission was not to "change tire after tire all day every day" or to "get a paycheck" or even to "avoid lawsuits for the boss." Their job was nothing less than to help people, like their own loved ones, to drive more safely. Their job was to save lives.

REAL LIFE: A professional fundraiser quit a position with a major national philanthropic organization because the organization's in-house legal department kept giving the fundraiser legal and procedural reasons for why the organization could not accept roughly twenty-five percent of the donations that she had successfully solicited while never offering advice regarding how donations could be legally accepted. Clearly, the Legal Department did not understand that their purpose was to help the non-profit to legally receive donations, not to obstruct them.

WHAT Excellent Organizations Do Differently

The management and staff of average organizations tend to focus on "me" and "money." Meanwhile, excellent organizations focus on noble, honorable, exciting goals. They provide a reason to be excited about going to work every day and feel proud of what you accomplished and contributed that day. Tire mechanics at average tire shops put tires on cars and get a paycheck.

Tire mechanics at excellent tire shops save lives. Excellent organizations not only have a goal and a mission; they mean it and live it, from the CEO to the janitor, from the staff that serves the public to those who work in the Legal Department.

WHY Excellent Organizations Do It Differently

Excellent organizations know that having a clear understanding of what your goal is, combined with having pride in and commitment to that goal, will create an enhanced motivation, energy and focus toward achieving that goal every day. Excellent organizations make a priority of creating such an environment so that all staff will contribute a more focused and inspired effort.

WHERE Is Your Organization Today?

Litmus Test #3 will help you to determine where your organization is today on the journey of providing a clear understood Mission to your Team.

LITMUS TEST #3: Mission

Complete here or download your free *Organization Whisperer Toolkit* from www.theorganizationwhisperer.com/kit. If your organization does not yet have a mission statement, then you will not be able to take this Litmus Test, but read it for your edification, then proceed to the "HOW" section to take the actions that will ripple your organization forward:

◉ E-mail at least twenty percent of your staff and ask them to e-mail back to you the organization's mission statement. Can they? Record the results and your observations here:

◉ E-mail a different twenty percent of staff and ask them to return to you their responses to the "Mission Litmus Test" worksheet included at the end of this chapter. Record results and observations here.

◉ Ask your management team to fill out and return to you their responses to the "Support Team" worksheet included at the end of this chapter. Record results and observations here:

Sample Mission Statements

"Southwest Airlines is dedicated to the highest quality of customer service delivered with warmth, friendliness, pride and company spirit."

"Google's mission is to organize the world's information and make it universally accessible and useful."

HOW to Become Excellent

Core Action #3 will help your organization create or fine-tune a clear inspirational mission.

CORE ACTION #3

✓ Form a Mission Statement Committee of the most appropriate staff (i.e the Cheerleaders, Succession Leadership Team, etc.) and assign this committee the task of creating an organizational mission statement or fine-tune the existing statement. Remind the committee that the best mission statements include the following elements:

- **Less than twelve words** so that it is easy to remember

- Includes focused **action verbs**, such as "give," "heal," "save"

- Includes words and **phrases unique to the organization**
  Example: Disney "makes magic," a seasoning company "spices up your life"

- **Vision**
  Example: the tire shop "saves lives;" an elementary school "develops the next generation"

- The Mission Statement Committee will meet:

  Date: _____   Time: _____

✓ Once the mission statement is complete, begin the process of positively, constructively implementing it, posting it, promoting it, meaning it, and living it throughout the organization on an ongoing basis. As you progress through this book and perform the ensuing nine core actions, a focus on the mission and its goals will automatically be one of the emanating ripples.

WHO Will Perform This Action

Constant focus on the Mission as the Organization's purpose will be provided by you and by the organizational cheerleaders that you identified in Core Action #1, the Succession Leadership Team that you identified in Core Action #2, and others that you feel would be great contributors to this Action.

Your Mission Statement Team will include:

1. _____
2. _____
3. _____
4. _____
5. _____

WHEN Will This Action Be Completed?

In Core Action #3 (above) you scheduled the Mission Statement Team to meet and finalize the Mission Statement on:

Date: _____ Time: _____

Once the Mission Statement is finalized and adopted, the immersion of "commitment to the mission" into the cultural fiber of the organization will be constantly re-enforced, fine-tuned, and improved. It will be modeled and emphasized every day.

The Organization Whisperer Toolkit
Mission Litmus Test

The Mission Litmus Test will help your organization fine-tune your existing Mission Statement or will guide you in the development of a quality brief, focused, inspiring Mission Statement. Complete here or download your free *Organization Whisperer Toolkit* from our website at www.theorganizationwhisperer.com/kit.

MISSION	
How do you rate your organization in the following best practices?	
BEST PRACTICE	**Rank from Lousy to Outstanding** 1__2__3__4__5__6__7__8__9__10
1. **BRIEF:** Board, staff easily recite the mission statement from heart.	
2. **FOCUSED:** The mission focuses and directs organizational behavior.	
3. **ALIGNED:** Employees can explain how their job contributes to achieving the Mission.	
4. **UNIQUE:** The mission honors the organization's unique purpose.	
5. **VISIONARY:** The mission provides a sense of purpose, worth, and value.	
TOTAL POINTS 5-15 Minimal 16-30 Somewhat 31-40 Advanced 41-50 Excellent	**SCORE**

The Organization Whisperer Toolkit
Support Teams

This tool will help you determine to what degree the six most common "support departments" are truly supporting and contributing to accomplishing your organization's mission, or to what degree some of them may not be contributing or may even be obstructing your organization's ability to perform with excellence and achieve its mission. Complete here or download your free *Organization Whisperer Toolkit* from our website: www.theorganizationwhisperer.com/kit.

SUPPORT TEAMS

To what degree do these six "Support Departments" contribute to, or obstruct, your Organization's ability to achieve its Mission and Goals?

BEST PRACTICE	Rank from Lousy to Outstanding 1__2__3__4__5__6__7__8__9__10
1. AUDIT	
2. BUDGET	
3. HUMAN RESOURCES	
4. INFORMATION TECHNOLOGY	
5. LEGAL	
6. PURCHASING	
TOTAL POINTS 6-18 Minimal 19-36 Somewhat 37-48 Advanced 49-60 Excellent	SCORE

Core Action #4—Family

Moving from Me to Team

Culture eats strategy for breakfast.

REAL LIFE: It is generally believed that the Great White Shark is the Lord of the Ocean, the biggest, baddest creature, feared by all. It could also be said that the Great White serves as the "poster boy" for many CEO's and Schools of Management; the symbol that they use as their philosophical compass. But the Great White does, in fact, fear one other force in the ocean: a family of dolphins.

A Great White knows that if it encounters a family of dolphins and does not retreat, the dolphin family turns into a fast, coordinated whirling dervish that delivers multiple non-stop head butts to the shark until it either retreats or dies from the incessant barrage. The true master of the oceans is not the lone, sociopathic killer; it is the smart, fast, coordinated dolphin family.

REAL LIFE: A child found an inexpensive, porcelain figurine of her favorite minor Disney character at a small gift kiosk in one of Disney World's theme parks. Her parents promised that they would buy it as they were leaving at the end of the day, so that it would not be broken during the day's activities, but they forgot. Upon returning to their Disney hotel in the afternoon the concierge alertly noticed that the child was upset and asked why.

When he was informed about the figurine, he asked for their hotel room number and which specific gift shop that they had seen it in. He said that he would take care of it and encouraged them to go enjoy the evening's fireworks show. Later, upon returning to their one hotel room out of thousands of Disney Hotel rooms, this one family out of thousands of families at Disney found the six-inch tall figurine laying on their daughter's pillow; a figurine made possible by an attentive, alert, caring concierge, a responsive Gift Shop and a committed delivery man . The smart, coordinated, fast Disney Family had once again accomplished their shared goal of "making magic."

WHAT Excellent Organizations Do Differently

In average organizations most of the staff is focused on what they can get out of the organization. Excellent organizations create a culture in which the staff focuses on how to constantly improve the organization. These organizations create a culture in which everyone works positively together to create a "purpose-focused family" atmosphere. The focus is on we, not me.

Excellent organizations successfully create and sustain their "we" cultures by prioritizing two core concepts. The first is NATURE, which relates to the organization's atmosphere, environment, and culture. The second is NURTURE, which focuses on the constructive development of the team's full potential.

Nature and Organizational Culture

Excellent organizations create and sustain "purpose-focused families" by "tapping into chi":

NATURE

Tradition

Atmosphere (CHI)

Purpose

Into Your Organization's

Creativity

Humanity

Integrity

1. **Tradition.** Successful organizations communicate and commemorate the organization's history of excellence. They constantly communicate stories about how the organization struggled early on but ultimately succeeded because of its outstanding innovations or quality customer service. Some organizations create a documentary of their illustrious history or have a Hall of Fame of their most admired and appreciated staff members.

2. **Atmosphere** (CHI). An organization's essence or soul — its chi or life force — is sustained in a working environment that, every day, encourages creativity, humanity, and integrity (more below).

3. **Purpose** (Mission, Goals). The importance of organizations having clearly defined and clearly understood purpose, mission, goals has already been discussed in Core Action #3, and you have probably already created and begun communicating your organization's mission.

4. *Into Your Organization's*

5. **Creativity.** Organizations that encourage and implement creativity are constantly adapting and improving. They are constantly in motion. Creativity is an organization's exercise. Excellent organizations understand that a creative environment is crucial not only to the organization's intellectual competitive edge but also to its edge in physical flexibility and adaptability.

6. **Humanity.** Excellent organizations value people, whether the people are their customers, their staff or their business partners. Their humanity is real, natural and ripples through their goals, their priorities, their decisions, their behavior.

7. **Integrity.**

> **FABLE:** Once there was a Queendom in which, at anytime that there was a job vacancy in the Castle, the Queen, known to the people as Queen Babe, would travel through the Queendom. On these travels, she would visit individually with citizens that the Queen believed could do a good job in the vacant position and she enthusiastically encouraged these citizens to apply. The Queen would tell them that her encouragement was not to be construed as a statement that she would select them but was only meant to indicate that she had noticed their excellent quality work and that she was certain that they would do a good job if they were to be selected.
>
> The Queen went to the citizens rather than summoning them to her and, face-to-face, she extended to them not a promise but an opportunity. Sincerely and honestly, she expressed her recognition of and appreciation of their quality work. Meanwhile, the neighboring King Napoleon grew jealous of the prosperity and happiness in the Queendom, so he ordered his ministers to modernize and become greater than the neighboring Queendom. His ministers built cardboard and plywood movie sets of modernized villages, dressed the serfs in nice clothes, and ordered them to stand on the Main Street of the kingdom and bow to the king as

he rode by. They then drove King Napoleon down Main Street in his carriage so that he could be pleased at all of the pretend progress in his kingdom.

Excellent organizations conduct themselves with integrity. People are treated with respect and honesty because they are truly valued and deserve to be treated with dignity. In average organizations, the leadership wants to be told what they want to hear. Leaders often do not truly care about the real health of the organization. In contrast, in excellent organizations, there is a sincere commitment to true, genuine excellence. Leaders of excellent organizations know that they cannot know the truth about the health of the organization unless the staff tells them the truth. They also know that the staff will not tell them the truth unless there is a sufficient comfort level that the leader will respond to the truth with humanity, civility, professionalism and true concern toward improving the organization.

Nurture and Organizational Culture

The specific actions that excellent organizations execute in order to create and sustain this desired culture of constant individual, team and organizational growth can be summarized in the following core elements of nurture:

NURTURE

Hire

Train

Count

Develop

Empower

Re-Focus

Reward

1. **Hiring.** Excellent organizations design recruitment, interview, and selection processes that prioritize and identify positive can-do personalities to attract employees who, by their presence, will contribute positive energy to the organization's chi and will be eager to enthusiastically learn and grow in the organization.

REAL LIFE: A new leader began his tenure in September. He encouraged his inherited staff to wear Halloween costumes on Halloween Day. Only the new leader and ten percent of the inherited staff did so. On the following Halloween, again only about ten percent of the inherited staff wore costumes, but of the new staff that the leader had hired during that year, eighty percent wore costumes, visual proof that the new leader had successfully maximized his opportunities to bring in new blood that rippled more enthused, positive, participative, and creative attitudes.

2. **Training.** Excellent organizations place a high priority on the initial training period. This training has three goals. First, it verifies to the new team member that this organization has a culture that is organized and professional and it expects them to adopt and live that culture. The second thing a strong training program does is it verifies to the new member that the organization is sincerely appreciative that they have joined the family. This is demonstrated by the organization's investment of considerable time and training materials into the new member's success. Third, the initial training is specifically designed to make the new member an effective contributor to some core functions in a short period of time.

3. **Count.**

FABLE: A chicken was outraged at her poor performance review score and berated the rooster for "picking on her." The rooster had anticipated how the meeting would go and had prepared a six-month "work produced" report which documented that the chicken had produced half as many eggs as any other chicken in the coop. The rooster slid the report across the table, allowed the chicken to review it, then asked if she had any further comments or questions. She did not.

Excellent organizations know that a new employee's development can be most accurately monitored and additional training and praise can be more accurately focused if quality of performance is measured. Such measurement may include tracking the number of requests filled, the number of customers served, or the number of errors made. The importance of counting and measurement will be discussed more thoroughly when we look at core action number eight.

4. Continued Development.

REAL LIFE: An organization interviewed a nineteen-year old young lady from a very deprived socio-economic background. She was uneducated and unsophisticated, but the organization decided to give her a chance because they liked her sincere "want to." On her first day, she showed up ready to go to work wearing her nightgown, slippers, and curlers in her hair, because she truly had no idea that this was unacceptable attire for work. She welcomed and willingly accepted the training that was offered. Two years later she had developed into an assistant manager.

Mediocre organizations may provide a bit of initial training for a week or two. Excellent organizations invest in the constant growth of their team members every day, forever. Constant improvement, both personally and professionally, is a part of the core fabric and culture of the organization.

5. Empowerment.

FABLE: Once a cow was brought to a new and unfamiliar pasture. This cow loved clover, so she watched the other cows for a few days until she noticed one cow who also loved clover. This cow seemed to know where all of the best clover was throughout the huge pasture. The new cow asked the "clover expert" if she could shadow her to learn where the best clover patches were.

Bull Napoleon overheard the conversation and chastised the new cow, saying, "You embarrassed me. Never do that again." The confused cow replied, "I am very sorry that I angered you. What did I do?" The bull huffily replied, "In front of my herd, you asked a question to someone other than me." The new cow replied, "Did you know the answer to my question?"

He replied, "No, that is not the point." The new cow replied, "Well, when I need a quality answer to a question, I ask the biggest expert, not the biggest ego."

REAL LIFE: A new leader took over an organization. He immediately e-mailed all staff and asked them for their "wish list" of improvements that they would like to see the organization implement. Of the list that the staff gave to him, he strategically prioritized ten recommendations that he felt he could actually get accomplished, would truly have a beneficial impact, and that would allow the staff to notice that their recommendations had been implemented. Through the year he issued updates on the progress toward implementation of those projects.

At the end of his first year, he again e-mailed all staff, reminding them that he had implemented all of the prioritized recommendations, thanked them for their innovative contributions to the organization, and asked them to submit more. This time he received twice as many suggestions.

While average organizations constantly consolidate responsibility into the hands or onto the desks of a few, excellent organizations are constantly driving tasks, functions, and responsibilities down the organization chart. They understand that to do so not only develops the next generation of leadership for the organization, but such empowerment also contributes to the everyday job satisfaction of front-line level employees by giving them job variety, responsibility, recognition, and a greater sense of worth.

In core action #2, you created and communicated an inspiring mission. In this chapter you have begun hiring and developing quality staff. Now is the time to prove that you have hired the right people and done a quality job of developing and inspiring them by turning them loose and supporting them as they accomplish great things. Enjoy watching their ripples of excellence expand. This is how excellent organizations do it.

6. Refocus.

REAL LIFE: We have all been in a building where a young child could be heard screaming all over the store. Invariably, when you see the child and his or her parent, the parent is either totally ignoring the child or is constantly repeating, "One more time…one more time!" In contrast, Mother Nature doesn't believe in "one more time" discipline. Mother Nature believes in swift and certain discipline.

If you swat a wasp nest, you know what the swift and certain punishment will be. If you walk up behind and startle a horse, you know what the swift and certain punishment will be. If you cannot swim but walk into the ocean, you know what the swift and certain punishment will be. Average organizations apply "one more time" discipline; excellent organizations apply Mother Nature's discipline.

REAL LIFE: A young man who had just been hired to work for Disney pulled into the parking lot and headed toward the building. A fellow worker with a pleasant smile pointed out to him a way in which he was violating the dress code. He corrected the issue, but, as he continued walking through the parking lot, a second co-worker pleasantly pointed out a second dress code offense.

The new employee, while still in the parking lot, had already learned that a part of the culture of excellent organizations is that they do not see rules as a form of punishment. Rather, they see rules as the foundation of pride. Mother Nature can provide breathtaking scenery, feed us, and care for us while also providing swift and certain discipline. Excellent organizations do the same.

Average organizations create a negative environment by constantly threatening staff ("one more time...") but never actually enforce any true standards. Excellent organizations constantly create a positive family environment but with the understanding that, should discipline be necessary, it is guaranteed, known, swift, and certain.

7. Reward.

FABLE: Once, when great Queen Babe was asked to share what she thought was the single most important key to her success, her reply was, "Every morning I put ten shillings in my purse and then walk around the kingdom. During the day, each time that I extend a compliment to a citizen for some contribution that I see them making to the kingdom, I thank them and give them a shilling. I do this until I have given away all ten shillings."

Excellent organizations constantly look for, notice, recognize, and reward excellent performance. Excellent organizations communicate a set of known performance goals, such as perfect attendance, balancing every day, and customer compliments. They issue known recognitions and rewards when a staff member achieves one of these goals.

It is important to note that the recognition is not based upon "who likes who," but is given when an employee has achieved known performance standards that contribute toward achieving the organization's mission. Recognition is also provided constantly, less formally, on a daily basis. This recognition constantly reminds staff that the goal is to contribute to the organization's success, that performance is being watched, and that it will be appreciated.

WHY Excellent Organizations Do It Differently

Smart, coordinated, and fast family-focused organizations have a long history of success, whether it is a family of dolphins against one shark, the Greeks against the behemoth Persians, the English navy against the mighty Spanish Armada, or the coordinated, united sports team defeating the one-star, me-dominated opponent.

Excellent organizations understand that this "family" culture creates numerous ripple benefits, including these seven results:

1. a more positive working environment,
2. increased loyalty and commitment,
3. less turnover,
4. increased accumulated knowledge and experience,
5. improved quality of customer service,
6. increased customer satisfaction, loyalty, return business, and "word of mouth," and
7. multiple smart, happy, dedicated, coordinated contributors to the organization are always better than one or none.

WHERE Is Your Organization Today?

Litmus Test #4 will help you determine where your organization is today on its journey from being me-focused to being team-focused.

LITMUS TEST #4: Team

Complete here or download your free *Organization Whisperer Toolkit* from our website at www.theorganizationwhisperer.com/kit.

◉ Of your organization's last five hires into management positions, how many of the five were developed and promoted from within the organization and how many were hired from outside the organization? Are the five newest managers an upgrade and improvement over the managers that they replaced? Record observations here:

◉ Does your organization's human resources (HR) director "get it?" Does the HR director understand and contribute to your organization's commitment to hiring new members of the organizational family who will work constructively together toward the organization's shared goal? Does your HR Director understand and contribute to nature and nurture, and TAPing into CHI? Record observations here:

◉ Take the "Empowerment LitmusTest" at the end of this chapter. How does your organization score? Record observations here:

◉ Take the attached "TAPing into CHI Litmus Test" at the end of this chapter. How does your organization score? Record observations here:

◉ Take the "PHACES Litmus Test" at the end of the chapter. How does your organization score? Record observations here:

HOW to Become Excellent

Core Action #4 will help your organization ripple from a "me" culture toward a "purpose-focused family" culture.

CORE ACTION #4

✓ Implement actions from the "TAPing into CHI Checklist" at the end of this chapter into your organization's culture.

✓ Implement actions from the "PHACES" Checklist at the end of this chapter into your organization's culture.

WHO Will Implement This Action?

Who, among the most respected staff members in the organization, would do the best job of injecting and sustaining (rippling) the TAPing into CHI and PHACES checklists throughout the organization?

Your Purpose-focused Family Team members will be:

1. _____

2. _____

3. _____

4. _____

5. _____

WHEN Will This Action Be Completed?

The immersion of TAPing into CHI and PHACES into the cultural fiber of the organization will be constantly re-enforced, fine-tuned, and improved. It must be consistently modeled and re-emphasized every day. The initial starter core actions need to be implemented immediately.

The first meeting of your Purpose-focused Family Team will be:

• Date: _____

• Time: _____

The Organization Whisperer Toolkit
The Empowerment Litmus Test

The Empowerment Litmus Test will assist you in determining how much of an empowered team culture your organization currently promotes. Complete here or download your free *Organization Whisperer Toolkit* from our website at www.theorganizationwhisperer.com/kit.

EMPOWERMENT	
How do you rate your organization in the following best practices?	
BEST PRACTICE	Rank from Lousy to Outstanding 1__2__3__4__5__6__7__8__9__10
1. This organization places a high priority on recruiting positive "Can Do" and empathetic "Service Focused" personalities.	
2. The interview and selection process includes participation by key staff from departments that will work directly with the person if hired.	
3. New employees are thoroughly oriented and trained in the organization's culture, mission, and processes.	
4. Professional development and personal growth are an important goal of the employee performance review process.	
5. Employee raises and promotions are based on positive attitudes, motivated commitment to the mission, and excellent performance.	
6. Organizational communication is open, honest, constructive, and mission focused.	
TOTAL POINTS 6-18 Minimal 19-36 Somewhat 37-48 Advanced 49-60 Excellent	**SCORE**

The Organization Whisperer Toolkit
TAPing into CHI Litmus Test

This worksheet will help you determine to what degree your organization has or has not yet maximized TAPing into your organization's CHI and created a purpose-focused family. Complete here or download your *Organization Whisperer Toolkit* online at www.theorganizationwhisperer.com/kit.

TAP into CHI	
GOAL	Rank from Lousy to Outstanding 1__2__3__4__5__6__7__8__9__10
Tradition	
Atmosphere (CHI)	
Purpose	
...into your organization's	
Creativity	
Humanity	
Integrity	
TOTAL POINTS 6-18 Minimal 19-36 Somewhat 37-48 Advanced 49-60 Excellent	**SCORE**

The Organization Whisperer Toolkit
PHACES Litmus Test

This worksheet will help you determine to what degree your organization has or has not yet: 1) prioritized hiring "PHACES" personality types, and 2) created an organizational culture that promotes and nurtures this constant development of PHACES behaviors. Complete here or download your free *Organization Whisperer Toolkit* from our website at www.theorganizationwhisperer.com/kit..

PHACES	
BEHAVIOR	**Degree to which it is lived.** 1__2__3__4__5__6__7__8__9__10
Positive	
Happy	
Alert	
Confident	
Energetic	
Sophisticated	
TOTAL POINTS 6-18 Minimal 19-36 Somewhat 37-48 Advanced 49-60 Excellent	**SCORE**

The Organization Whisperer Toolkit
TAPing into CHI Checklist

Use this checklist to implement actions to support your organization in tapping into its chi. Complete here or download your free *Organization Whisperer Toolkit* at www.theorganizationwhisperer.com/kit.

TAP into CHI	
GOAL	**SPECIFIC ACTION**
Tradition	Ask staff or retirees to share two stories from the organization's past
	Select two or three stories to share with all staff
	Include stories in "Welcoming New Team Members" materials
Atmosphere (CHI)	See Chi Below
Purpose	The Mission Statement
...into your organization's	
Creativity	Prioritize hiring creative people (see "PHACES Interview Questions" and "PHACES Interview Analysis Sheet")
	See Chapter 9 "Processes"
Humanity	Hire staff that possesses professional humanity (see "PHACES Interview Questions" and "PHACES Interview Analysis Sheet")
	Challenge yourself to model professional humanity
Integrity	Hire staff that possesses integrity (see "PHACES Interview Questions" and "PHACES Interview Analysis Sheet")
	Prioritize and model integrity

The Organization Whisperer Toolkit
PHACES Checklist

This checklist will provide direction as you strengthen your organization's commitment to hiring, developing, and nurturing PHACES personality traits. Complete here or download your free *Organization Whisperer Toolkit* from our website at www.theorganizationwhisperer.com/kit.

PHACES Checklist	
GOAL	**SPECIFIC ACTION**
FIRST	Form a "Faculty" of Appropriate Staff To Lead All Aspects of PHACES University
HIRE	Use the "PHACES Interview Questions" and the "PHACES Interview Analysis" Checklists
TRAIN	Use the "Welcoming New Team Members" and the "Training Materials" Checklists
COUNT	See Chapter 8 (Measure)
DEVELOP	Develop "Mission and Me" Task, Grow, and Improve Goals With Each Staff Member
EMPOWER	Fill Out "Empowerment" Worksheets, then See Chapter 9 (Processes)
REFOCUS	Based Upon Measurable and Documentable Data, Identify Least Contributive and Cooperative 5% of Staff
REFOCUS	Prepare and Discuss "Mission and Me" Improvement Goals and Dates With Them
REWARD	Determine 3-5 "Most Desired" Performance Standards (Attendance, No Errors, Customer Compliments, etc.) and Reward Monthly or Quarterly Staff Who Exceed Standards
REWARD	Express Appreciation to 10% of Staff Each Day

The Organization Whisperer Toolkit
PHACES Interview Questions

This interview aid will assist you in better identifying PHACES personalities who will be more likely to be contributors to the purpose-focused family. Complete here or download your free *Organization Whisperer Toolkit* from our website at www.theorganizationwhisperer.com/kit.

PHACES Interview Questions

BEFORE THE INTERVIEW

Place a piece of "paper trash" on the floor by the Receptionist and see if the Applicant:
1) picks up and throws away the trash, and/or 2) speaks pleasantly with the Receptionist.

Seat the Applicant in front of a poster of the Office Mission Statement. During the Interview you will ask them about it, to see if they even noticed or thought about it.

INTERVIEW QUESTIONS

1) If you could change one thing about "most people," what would it be and why?

2) What was the best gift that you ever got? Gave?

3) If a movie was made about your life, who would play you?
   Describe three important scenes.

4) On a scale of 1-10, how lucky are you? Why do you think so?

5) On a scale of 1-10, how weird are you? Why do you think so?

6) Tell us about a failure that you have experienced and what you learned from it?

7) What gets you excited about starting each day?

8) One year from now, what do you hope to have accomplished in your life?

9) What is something that you believe which most people disagree with?

10) What does our organization's mission statement mean to you?

11) Tell us about your last 3 jobs? Last 3 supervisors?

The Organization Whisperer Toolkit
PHACES Interview Analysis

Complete from this page or download your free *Organization Whisperer Toolkit* online at www.theorganizationwhisperer.com/kit..

PHACES Interview Analysis

POSITIVE

Negative 1 2 3 4 5 6 7 8 9 10 Positive

Defeatist 1 2 3 4 5 6 7 8 9 10 Constructive

Can't Do 1 2 3 4 5 6 7 8 9 10 Let's Do

COMMENTS:

HAPPY

Unhappy 1 2 3 4 5 6 7 8 9 10 Happy

Pessimistic 1 2 3 4 5 6 7 8 9 10 Optimistic

Complainer 1 2 3 4 5 6 7 8 9 10 Upbeat

Blamer 1 2 3 4 5 6 7 8 9 10 Responsible

COMMENTS:

ALERT

Lethargic 1 2 3 4 5 6 7 8 9 10 Attentive

Distracted 1 2 3 4 5 6 7 8 9 10 Focused

COMMENTS:

CONFIDENT

Insecure 1 2 3 4 5 6 7 8 9 10 Relaxed

Arrogant 1 2 3 4 5 6 7 8 9 10 Humble

Bombastic 1 2 3 4 5 6 7 8 9 10 Understated

COMMENTS:

ENERGETIC											
Listless	1	2	3	4	5	6	7	8	9	10	Motivated
Discouraged	1	2	3	4	5	6	7	8	9	10	Purposeful
Hyper	1	2	3	4	5	6	7	8	9	10	Enthusiastic
Distracted	1	2	3	4	5	6	7	8	9	10	Focused
COMMENTS:											

SOPHISTICATED											
Poor Communication	1	2	3	4	5	6	7	8	9	10	Fluent
Flawed Thought	1	2	3	4	5	6	7	8	9	10	Sound Reasoning
Crude Demeanor	1	2	3	4	5	6	7	8	9	10	Civility
COMMENTS:											

The Organization Whisperer Toolkit
Welcome New Employees Checklist

The checklist that follows will guide you in developing a quality Welcome Kit for new staff members which will send them a first impression regarding the organization's culture of excellence. Complete here or download your free *Organization Whisperer Toolkit* from our website at www.theorganizationwhisperer.com/kit.

#1   Welcome them to the organization.

#2   Introduce them to team members and supervisors.

#3   Introduce them to their mentor star.

#4   Explain how their duties will contribute to the mission.

#5   Discuss their specific performance goals.

#6   Give them their training materials and discuss them.

#7   Review employee handbook. Discuss policies and benefits.

#8   Check in on them and their mentor for two weeks.

The Organization Whisperer Toolkit

Training Materials Checklist

Complete here or download your free *Organization Whisperer Toolkit* from our website at www.theorganizationwhisperer.com/kit.

#1 Key words, phrases, and meanings

#2 Key forms

#3 Key functions, tasks, and processes

#4 Key computer programs

#5 Key customer questions and requests

#6 Key deadlines (reports, laws, and rules)

#7 Key fees

#8 Key cross-references

The Organization Whisperer Toolkit

Mission and Me

Complete here or download your free *Organization Whisperer Toolkit* from our website at this page: www.theorganizationwhisperer.com/kit.

MISSION AND ME

The Mission:

Me (Name):

My Tasks / Contributions:

How I Can Grow:

Why I Need to Grow:

Specific Growth Goals:

Specific Dates to Achieve Goals:

The Organization Whisperer Toolkit
Empowerment Contribution Worksheet

These worksheets will guide you in innovating ways that specific team members can be called upon to better contribute their talents to the organization. Complete here or download your free *Organization Whisperer Toolkit* from our website at www.theorganizationwhisperer.com/kit.

EMPOWERING INDIVIDUALS. List five employees and their unique talent(s) that could be empowered to benefit the organization.

Name	Talent(s)	Contribution(s)
Sue Picasso	Artistic	Paint a mural in break room
Bob	Spanish speaking	Translate documents and conversations

Name	Talent(s)	Contribution(s)

EMPOWERING TEAMS. Create teams whose coordinated talents could benefit the organization.

Team	Talent(s)	Team Project
Sara	Sales/Marketing	Review organizational marketing materials and redesign them to more clearly represent customer programs and services.
John	Copywriting	
Tran	Project Management	
Becky	Printing, Graphics	

Team A	Talent(s)	Team Project

Team B	Talent(s)	Team Project

Core Action #5— Decisions

Moving from Re-Active to Reasoned Pro-Activity

Eighty percent of businesses fail within ten years. The U.S. Federal Government is trillions of dollars in debt. The majority of marriages fail. Clearly, most people and organizations could improve the quality of their decision-making.

FABLE: Quite a few years ago a chicken kept telling everyone that the sky was about to fall, but it never did. One afternoon the chicken decided to try to learn in what ways her decision-making could be improved. On review, she realized that she always felt that the sky would fall on a Friday, at the end of a challenging week on Napoleon's poverty stricken farm. In short, she was making and announcing bad decisions when she was tired and frustrated. The sky wasn't literally falling, she only felt like it was or even wished it was.

REAL LIFE: Several years ago there was an excellent television commercial in which an office team was meeting in the conference room to try and solve a challenge. In the commercial, a middle-aged balding frumpy guy speaks up with a solution which everyone dismisses. Thirty seconds later, the young hunky guy in the Italian suit repeats exactly what the frumpy guy had said and everyone hails him as brilliant.

FABLE: Once there was a rabbit in a race with a tortoise. The rabbit made a decision that he could stop, take a nap, then still easily win the race. However, he made a poorly considered decision regarding for how long he could nap and, consequently, suffered one of the great upsets in racing history; not due to a lack of talent but due to a lack of sophisticated decision-making skills.

WHAT Excellent Organizations Do Differently

There are eight key behaviors or ripples that excellent organizations prioritize in their decision-making processes. In this chapter and the next two chapters you will sequentially utilize these eight ripples. These behaviors which ripple out into excellence include:

- **ANTICIPATE**, which allows these organizations to initiate and plan their decision-making process in a calm, reasoned atmosphere rather than constantly and hastily reacting to the unexpected emergency of the moment.

- **IDENTIFY**, not just the surface-level perceived problem, which is the tip of the iceberg, but the deeper, core root cause of this problem.

- **INCLUDE** all parties who have expertise and a vested interest in the particular challenge, issue, or process that is being analyzed.

- **RECOGNIZE** not just the core challenge, but all of the additional (ripple) processes, people, resources, and partners that this particular challenge impacts.

- **INNOVATE** not just an obvious short-term, band-aid solution but an innovative long-term improvement to the organization. Remember, a crisis is a terrible opportunity to waste.

- **PRIORITIZE** decisions that achieve the organization's mission, not decisions that pass the buck or promote personal careers.

- **IMPLEMENT.** While mediocre organizations usually decide to totally ignore an issue or merely talk about it, excellent organizations actually implement innovative solutions.

- **FOLLOW-UP.** Mediocre organizations have a mindset that a decision to implement is a final "huge" decision and that the new processes and rules will be written in stone forever. Therefore, these mediocre organizations believe that solutions cannot be implemented until they are perfectly designed, because they might never be revisited. Conversely, excellent organizations have a culture of constant improvement, deciding in one small step to implement something today, then in another small step to monitor and improve tomorrow, and in yet another small step to monitor and decide to tweak again the next day. While mediocre organizations tend to terminate implementations that struggle in order to protect their façade of perfection, excellent organizations reward constant efforts toward incremental improvement.

In this chapter and the ensuing two chapters you will utilize these eight behaviors.

WHY Excellent Organizations Do It Differently

Excellent organizations believe in building a house of bricks rather than a house of straw. These organizations believe in recycling a can rather than kicking it down the road. They believe in making tomorrow better rather than making excuses today.

WHERE Is Your Organization Today?

Litmus Test #5 will help you determine where your organization is today on the journey from reactively making quick and possibly emotional decisions to pro-actively making well-considered decisions.

LITMUS TEST #5: Decisions

Consider the following questions to evaluate where your organization is today on the continuum between reactive and reasoned pro-active decisions. Complete here or download your free *Organization Whisperer Toolkit* from our website at www.theorganizationwhisperer.com/kit.

- ⦿ Identify all of the important decisions that your organization has made during the past six months. List them below, then consider the questions which follow and include your reflections below each question.

1. _____

2. _____

3. _____

4. _____

5. _____

6. _____

- ⦿ How many of these decisions were successful?

- ⦿ Why were these decisions successful?

- ⦿ How many failed?

- ⦿ Why do you believe these decisions failed?

⦿ How could all of the decisions, both successes and failures, have been improved even more?

Compare and reconcile the answers that you gave here with the answers that you gave to similar questions in Litmus Test #2. Make note of the areas for improvement that Litmus Tests #2 and #5 have identified.

HOW to Become Excellent

Core Action #5 will ripple your organization from making re-active decisions toward pro-actively developing well-considered reasoned decisions.

CORE ACTION #5

✓ **ANTICIPATE** the three most beneficial decisions that your organization should be making right now. Consider low-risk and high reward actions that will quickly and easily produce fairly high impact results. List these below:

    1. _____

    2. _____

    3. _____

You may wish to compare and reconcile the answers that you gave here with the answers that you gathered from the organization's staff in Core Action #2.

✓ **IDENTIFY** the true core challenge that should be targeted within each of these three issues by analyzing them with the assistance of the "Identify (3-Why) Your Core Challenge" worksheet at the end of the chapter.

In the next two core action chapters, which involve planning and doing, you will use the remaining six recommended behaviors that were introduced in this chapter.

WHO Will Perform This Action?

The action of anticipating and accurately identifying opportunities to improve your organization provides a constructive opportunity to develop your Succession Planning Team members.

Members of Your Succession Planning Team:

1. _____
2. _____
3. _____
4. _____
5. _____

WHEN Will This Action Be Completed?

Remember that the first thing that excellent organizations do differently is they pro-actively anticipate opportunities to improve. Schedule a Succession Planning Team meeting so that they can do so.

Our Opportunities for Improvement Anticipation and Identification Meeting will be:

- Date: _____

- Time: _____

P.S. Remember the rabbit.

The Organization Whisperer Toolkit
Identify (3-Why) Your Core Challenge

Complete here or download your free *Organization Whisperer Toolkit* from our website at www.theorganizationwhisperer.com/kit.

3-WHY CORE CHALLENGE IDENTIFIER

WHAT do you believe to be the challenge?

WHO experiences it or notices it occurring?

WHEN does it occur?

WHY does it occur? (**WHY 1**)

Why does **THAT** (above) occur? (**WHY 2**)

Why does **THAT** (above) occur? (**WHY 2**)

Why does **THAT** (above) occur? (**WHY 3**)

Does it appear you have identified the true **CORE CHALLENGE**(s)?
If so, congrats! If not, keep asking **WHY**.

WHAT have you now identified as the core challenge?

WHAT are some of the ripple impacts of this core challenge?

Impact #1:

Impact #2:

Impact #3:

Impact #4:

Impact #5:

Core Action #6—Plan

Moving from No Planning to Daily Planning

Have you ever noticed that the same people and the same organizations seem to repeatedly get lucky? Repeated luck is created in environments of constant preparation combined with constant alertness for opportunity.

Plan = What x How x Who x When

FABLE: Once there were Three Little Pigs who happened to live in a dangerous forest environment that was full of wolves. One day a wolf blew down the first little pig's straw hut and ate him. Then the wolf moved on, blew down the second little pig's twig hut and ate that little pig. Then the wolf moved on again, but he must have gotten tired along the way because by the time he got to the home of the third little pig, he was apparently out of breath and could not blow down the third little pig's brick castle. What a lucky little pig.

WHAT Excellent Organizations Do Differently

Excellent organizations constantly ask their staff, partners, customers, and outside experts, "How can we improve?" They maintain a constantly evolving list of new Opportunities For Improvement (OFI's) that range from major restructuring to seemingly insignificant tweaks.

WHY Excellent Organizations Do It Differently

Excellent organizations understand that their options are to constantly improve or to die. Mediocre organizations attempt to delude themselves that sameness and constancy can be sustained. Mediocrity and sameness have never succeeded for very long, whether in nature or among humans, nations, or organizations. Great organizations motivate themselves with the understanding that long-term survival is possible only by staying one step ahead — smarter, faster, and/or stronger — of the competition in the survival struggle for life-giving resources, whether that be oxygen, water, food, customers, or money.

WHERE Is Your Organization Today?

Litmus Test #6 will help you determine where your organization is today on the journey from no planning toward constant, effective planning.

LITMUS TEST #6: Plan

Take the "Improving Organization Diagnostic" at the end of the chapter. Complete here or download your free *Organization Whisperer Toolkit* from our website at www.theorganizationwhisperer.com/kit. As a result of taking the diagnostic test, consider these questions and record your answers below:

In what ways is our organization doing well?

In what areas can we improve?

HOW to Become Excellent

Core Action #6 will help ripple your organization toward a culture of constant constructive planning.

CORE ACTION #6

✓ **DISTRIBUTE** "The Adrenaline Rush" and "The Idea Incubator" worksheets at the end of the chapter, making sure to INCLUDE (Decision-making Ripple #3) all staff, key partners, key vendors, and key customers. Solicit their feedback and recommendations.

✓ **COMBINE** these recommendations that are submitted with the three "most beneficial decisions" that you identified in Core Action #5, and use the "OFI's Planning Kit" worksheet at the end of this chapter to help you complete the following three tasks.

✓ **RECOGNIZE** (Decision-making Ripple #4) not just the core issue being addressed, but also all related impacts,

✓ **INNOVATE** (Decision-making Ripple #5) not quick patches but long-term innovative advancements, and

✓ **PRIORITIZE** (Decision-making Ripple #6) the recommended innovations that create the most "bang for the buck" and have the highest cost-benefit ratio toward better achieving the mission.

For now, place higher priority on quicker, easier-to-implement, and favorable cost-benefit ratio projects, so that you can implement more projects, establish a high success rate, and thereby send the message that successfully implementing innovative improvements has become a high priority in the new organizational culture.

WHO Will Perform This Action

You will perform this action with the support of your Succession Team.

Your Succession Team includes the following members:

1. _____
2. _____
3. _____
4. _____
5. _____

WHEN Will This Action Be Completed?

The *Adrenaline Rush* and the *Idea Incubator* Worksheets will be distributed:

- Date / Time: _____

And the deadline to return them to you for review will be:

- Date/Time: _____

The *OFI's Planning Kit* Will Be Completed By:

- Date / Time: _____

The Organization Whisperer Toolkit
Improving Organization Diagnostic

This Litmus Test will help you determine where your organization is currently on its journey toward becoming a constantly planning organization. Complete here or download your free *Organization Whisperer Toolkit* from our website at www.theorganizationwhisperer.com/kit.

ADAPT	
How do you rate your organization in the following best practices?	
BEST PRACTICE	**Rank from Lousy to Outstanding** 1 2 3 4 5 6 7 8 9 10
1. A strategic planning retreat of the full board and key staff is held annually.	
2. Employees are empowered to participate in the strategic planning process and are involved in implementation.	
3. 75% or more of strategic plan objectives are successfully implemented within two years.	
4. More time, staff, and resources are invested in pursuing pro-active improvements than in re-acting to unanticipated challenges.	
5. Strategic planning and prioritizing of implementation are driven by how to better achieve the mission.	
6. Strategic implementations and their measurable impacts are tracked and transparently reported monthly or quarterly.	
7. Creativity, experimentation, and learning from failures are encouraged, recognized, and rewarded.	
TOTAL POINTS 7-21 Minimal 22-42 Somewhat 43-56 Advanced 57-70 Excellent	**SCORE**

The Organization Whisperer Toolkit
Adrenaline Rush

Complete here or download your free *Organization Whisperer Toolkit* from our website at www.theorganizationwhisperer.com/kit. This worksheet will provide your staff, partners, vendors, and customers with thought triggers to help them identify organizational opportunities for improvement.

ADRENALIN (CHALLENGE)	RUSH (INNOVATIONS)
BACKLOGS (WHY?) 1) 2)	1) 2)
CUSTOMER COMPLAINTS (WHY?) 1) 2)	1) 2)
EMPLOYEE COMPLAINTS (WHY?) 1) 2)	1) 2)
EMPLOYEE TURNOVER (WHY?) 1) 2)	1) 2)
HIGH RESOURCE USE (IMPROVE) 1) 2)	1) 2)
HIGH VOLUME FUNCTIONS (IMPROVE) 1) 2)	1) 2)
MISSED DEADLINES (WHY?) 1) 2)	1) 2)

SUGGESTIONS OF MGMT/STAFF (IMPROVE) 1) 2)	1) 2)
POOR COMPARITIVE MEASURES (IMPROVE) 1) 2)	1) 2)
ADDITIONAL OPPORTUNITIES 1) 2)	1) 2)

The Organization Whisperer Toolkit
Idea Incubator

This worksheet provides your teams, partners, and vendors with thought triggers to help them identify organizational opportunities for improvement. Complete here or download your free *Organization Whisperer Toolkit* from our website at www.theorganizationwhisperer.com/kit.

IDEA INCUBATOR

1. COMMUNICATIONS / SIGNAGE / TELEPHONES / WEBSITE (See Action #1): How can the quality of office communications be improved?

A.

B.

2. ENVIRONMENT (See Action #4): Suggestions to make the organization a purpose-focused family.

A.

B.

3. EQUIPMENT (See Action #10): Suggestions on improving office equipment.

A.

B.

4. FORMS/SCREENS (See Actions #1 and #9): How can our paper forms and/or computer screens be improved?

A.

B.

5. **LAWS/REGULATIONS** (See Action #11): Are there laws/regulations that are obstructive and should be amended; or laws/regulations that, if implemented, would be helpful?

A.

B.

6. **PARTNERSHIPS** (See Action #11): How could current interactions be improved, streamlined? New partnership opportunities?

A.

B.

7. **SPACE:** Suggestions on how to more effectively maximize available space.

A.

B.

8. **SUPPLIES** (See Action #10): Can the availability and distribution of needed supplies be improved?

A.

B.

9. **TECHNOLOGY** (See Actions #1, #9, #10)(Computers, faxes, copiers, Internet, etc.): Recommendations on how technology can contribute toward better achieving the mission.

A.

B.

10.TRAINING (See Action # 4): How could staff training and development be improved?

A.

B.

11.MISCELLANEOUS: What are other ways to improve the organization and better achieve the mission?

A.

B.

The Organization Whisperer Toolkit
OFI's Planning Kit

The OFI Planning Kit will help you recognize, innovate and prioritize new opportunities for improvement within your organization. Complete here or download your free *Organization Whisperer Toolkit* from our website at www.theorganizationwhisperer.com/kit.

IDENTIFY	RECOGNIZE	INNOVATE	PRIORITIZE
3-Why OFIs (include invested parties)	Ripple Impacts	Long-term Improvements	Mission-focused Bang for Buck

Core Action #7—Do

Moving from Procrastination to Done Today

*There are those who make things happen, those who
watch things happen, and those who say "What happened?"*

REAL LIFE: A large, international hotel chain had a culture in which every staff member worldwide was encouraged to e-mail their suggestions directly to the CEO. A janitor in one hotel e-mailed his recommendation that all cigarette ash trays should have black rather than white sand because black sand would not look as dirty and would not have to be replaced as often. Within ten days, every ash tray at every hotel worldwide in that chain had black sand.

FABLE: Once a Little Pig was walking through the woods and encountered a Wolf. He told the Wolf about how for the past 3 years he had meant to build a brick castle. The Wolf ate him.

WHAT Excellent Organizations Do Differently

Great organizations have an 80-80-Percent Rule: They want to be spending at least eighty percent of their time initiating, innovating, and implementing improvements while spending less than twenty percent of their time having to react to the unforeseen ; and these organizations want to successfully implement at least eighty percent of quality recommendations within one year of the initial recommendation.

WHY Excellent Organizations Do It Differently

Great organizations know that survival doesn't happen by ignoring, planning or promising; it happens by doing. They also know that staff will continue to innovate only as long as they actually see that their innovations are being implemented.

WHERE Is Your Organization Today?

Litmus Test #7 will help you determine where your organization is today on the journey from procrastinating to doing.

LITMUS TEST #7: Do

Complete here or download your free *Organization Whisperer Toolkit* from our website at www.theorganizationwhisperer.com/kit.

◉ In the past month how much time has your organization spent planning, innovating, and implementing as opposed to reacting? Is your organization at the eighty percent threshold?

◉ Over the past year, how many OFI's has your organization's staff innovated?

◉ How many of those innovations have been implemented ? At least eighty percent?

HOW to Become Excellent

Core Action #7 will ripple your organization toward placing a higher priority on quickly implementing organizational improvement.

CORE ACTION #7

✓ Place the top five OFI's that you prioritized in the "OFI's Planning Kit" in the previous chapter onto the "Do It-Action / Date Certain Implementation" worksheet you will find at the end of this chapter.

✓ Complete the remainder of the "Do It-Action/Date Certain Implementation" worksheet (Decision-Making Ripple #7).

✓ Follow up (Decision-Making Ripple #8) is the next step. Monitor and Measure the specific, planned steps of the implementations as documented on your "Do It" worksheet.

WHO Will Perform This Action

Refresh your memory by referring to the "WHO" column of the "Do It" worksheet and reminding yourself who the identified Project Leaders are. Then, create five implementation teams, one for each of the five prioritized opportunities for improvement (OFIs). Each team should be composed of the impacted experts within your organization, the staff who are most vested in the outcome and will be the most impacted by the implementation of that particular OFI.

WHEN Will This Action Be Completed?

Complete this core action according to the "Dates Certain" targeted on the "Do It" worksheet. Hopefully, project completions will occur before you encounter the Wolf.

The Organization Whisperer Toolkit
Do It-Action / Date Certain Implementation

This Organization Whisperer tool will help you organize and quickly implement the actions needed in order to improve your organization. Complete here or download your free *Organization Whisperer Toolkit* from our website at www.theorganizationwhisperer.com/kit.

WHAT	WHO	HOW	WHEN	FOLLOW-UP	IMPACT MEASURES
Top Prioritized OFIs	Will Implement	Specific Steps Toward Implementation	Date for Completion of Each Step	How's It Going? Adapt and Fine-Tune	Before & After Performance Measures
#1-					
#2-					
#3-					
#4-					
#5-					

The Organization Whisperer Toolkit
From Concept to Implementation

From Concept to Implementation
Avoid this!

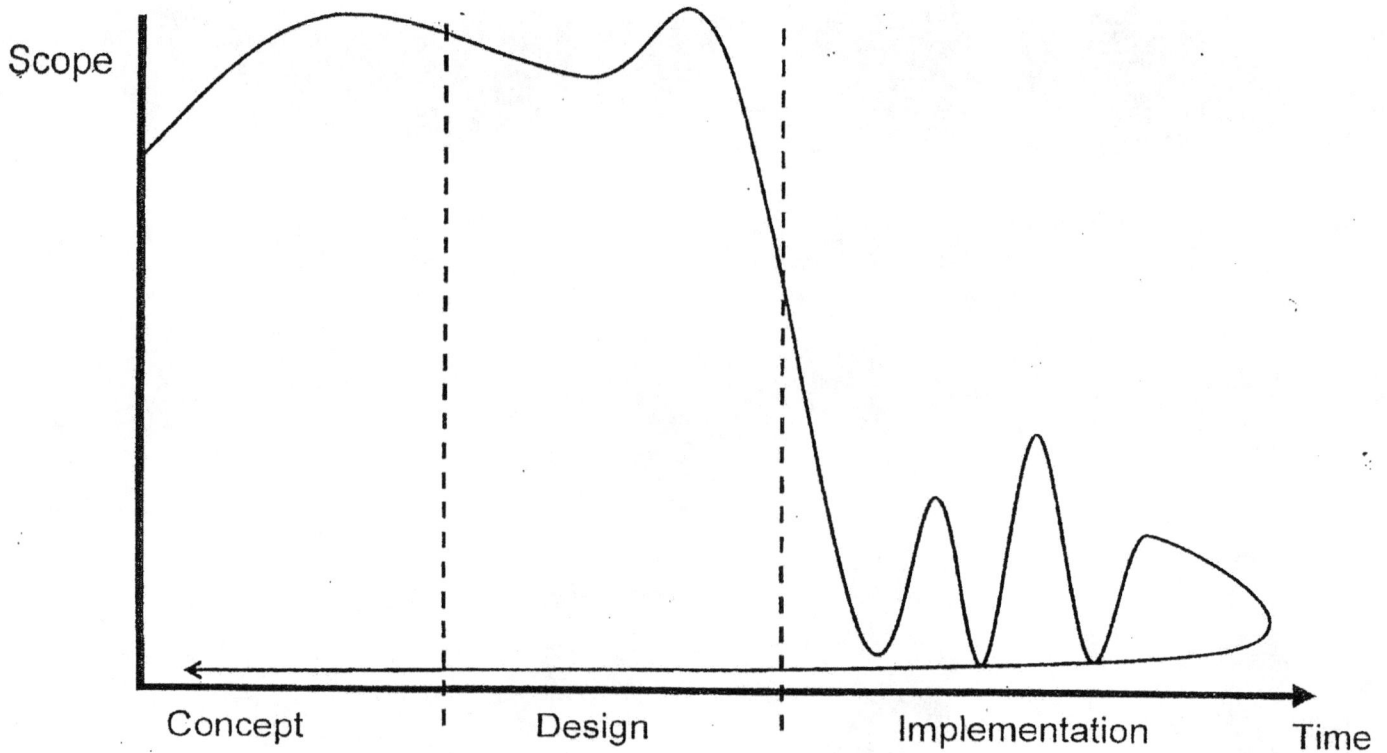

The Organization Whisperer Toolkit
Six Phases of a Project

1   Enthusiasm

2   Disillusionment

3   Panic

4   Search for the Guilty

5   Punishment of the Innocent

6   Praise and Honor for Non-Participants

Core Action #8—Measure

Moving from No Measurement to Daily Measurement

What gets measured gets done.

REAL LIFE: A young man, working out in a gym, plans to do fifty sit-ups. As he completes forty sit-ups, a beautiful young woman gets on a nearby treadmill and, as she jogs, she begins to watch him. He does 114 sit-ups.

REAL LIFE: Following the announcement that a choice of a jar of peanuts or a bottle of bubble bath would be given for meeting monthly performance goals, the number of staff achieving their goals improved from three to twenty in an organization of forty-one staff members.

WHAT Excellent Organizations Do Differently

Great organizations prioritize measuring performance and do so constantly. They recognize and reward excellent performance. They measure three to seven most critical core efficiencies and outcomes. In organizations committed to excellence, all staff engage in constant discussion about how to improve in those three to seven categories, which creates holistic cooperation and constant improvement across all facets of the organization. The performance management culture of excellent organizations is positive and progressive, not punitive.

REAL LIFE: A telephone unit that had an average customer wait time of eight minutes and 41 seconds and an average call abandonment rate of 48 percent kept asking for additional staff. Instead, a performance monitoring program was implemented in which the staff was informed that goals would be set for attendance, average length of call, and quality of call (which would be determined by live call monitoring). In addition, the staff was informed that for each month that they met or exceeded the performance standards they would receive bonus pay. Attendance improved by twelve percent, the number of calls answered increased by a third, and average customer wait time decreased from eight minutes 41 seconds to three minutes 21 seconds. In addition, abandoned calls decreased from 48 percent to 22 percent. This improvement in performance was achieved with the same staff members.

WHY Excellent Organizations Do It Differently

REAL LIFE: A data entry staff, upon learning that their number of keystrokes was being counted, increased their number of keystrokes by 30 percent.

Excellent organizations know that performance management cultures consistently perform 25 to 40 percent more efficiently and productively than other organizations, as cited by the Gallup Poll that was discussed in Core Action #1.

WHERE Is Your Organization Today?

Litmus Test #8 will help you determine where your organization is today on the journey toward sustaining a performance management culture.

LITMUS TEST #8: Measure

Complete here or download your free *Organization Whisperer Toolkit* from our website at www.theorganizationwhisperer.com/kit.

◉ What are your organization's three to seven core performance measures?

1. _____
2. _____
3. _____
4. _____
5. _____
6. _____
7. _____

◉ How much has organizational performance improved in the past year?

◉ Can you document this improvement?

◉ Who are the "gold standard" benchmark organizations in your profession?

⦿ How do your organization's performance measures compare to the benchmark's measures?

⦿ Who are your three to five most productive staff members?

1. _____
2. _____
3. _____
4. _____
5. _____

⦿ Which specific measures do you use to document and verify staff performance?

1. _____
2. _____
3. _____
4. _____
5. _____

HOW to Become Excellent

Core Action #8 will ripple your organization toward a more sophisticated performance-based culture.

CORE ACTION #8

Complete here or download your free *Organization Whisperer Toolkit* from our website at www.theorganizationwhisperer.com/kit.

✓ Ask staff to use the "Core Measures Development Worksheet" at the end of this chapter to provide them direction in creating measures that will help them measure, document and verify:
1) their personal performance, 2) the performance of their department, 3) the degree to which organizational performance is improving, 4) their department's performance compared to benchmark departments, and 5) how well the organization is successfully achieving its mission.

✓ Analyze, synthesize, and adapt the submitted proposed measures into three to seven core measures that can, together, provide insight into the holistic performance of the organization.

1. _____
2. _____
3. _____
4. _____
5. _____
6. _____
7. _____

✓ Create the processes necessary in order to be able to quickly and easily gather the data for the three to seven core measures. Keep in mind that it should take no longer than one hour per month to create the organization's monthly Core Measures Report.

WHO Will Perform This Action

You, with the assistance of staff members who you feel could provide detailed holistic organizational knowledge and insight toward creating the most effectively targeted measures, and / or who might provide assistance with creating the data gathering processes.

Your Measurement Team:

1. _____
2. _____
3. _____
4. _____
5. _____

WHEN Will This Action Be Completed?

An initial set of three to seven core measures and data gathering processes can be created within a week. The measures can be tweaked and fine-tuned in the future as needed. The Measurement Team will finalize creating a package of three to seven core holistic measures and will develop the efficient data gathering processes.

Measurement Team Report Due Date:

- Date: _____
- Time: _____

The Organization Whisperer Toolkit
Core Measures Development Worksheet

The "Core Measures Development" tool assists you in identifying core measures for your organization. Complete here or download your free *Organization Whisperer Toolkit* from our website at www.theorganizationwhisperer.com/kit.

MEASUREMENT PRIORITIES	MEASURES
Chronic Backlogs and Missed Deadlines	
Employee Turnover and Complaints	
Errors	
Highly Repetitive Processes and Functions	
High Resource Use Processes and Functions	
Quality of Customer Service and Satisfaction	
Technology Upgrades and Enhancements	
Comparative Measures (Trends, Benchmarks, Competition)	
Other Perceived Strengths	
Other Perceived Weaknesses	

Your Core Measures Might Focus On:

INPUTS	OUTPUTS	OUTCOMES	EFFICIENCY	QUALITY
People	*# Served*	*Revenue*	*Time*	*Accuracy*
Resources	*# Products*	*Improvement*	*Cost*	*On Time*
Funding	*# Events*	*Benefits*	*Process*	*In Budget*
Facility	*# Services*	*Impact*		*Satisfaction*
Materials				*Referrals*

Core Action #9—Processes

Moving from "We Always Have Done It This Way" to "Here's a Better Way"

Smarter, faster, easier . . . constantly.

REAL LIFE: An organization had been using 15-digit identification codes for their products. They developed and converted to a 6-digit code, which saved roughly seven seconds every time that they entered the data or spoke the code. The conversion also reduced errors caused by misunderstandings of spoken codes ("Did you say 5-0 or five zeroes?"). It reduced data entry errors and reduced the time invested in correcting such errors. The organization estimated that the time saved just in the seven seconds saved reciting the shorter code during telephone communications added up to one person-week every two months.

WHAT Excellent Organizations Do Differently

Excellent organizations constantly, relentlessly, daily try to innovate and implement smarter, faster, and easier processes. This ranges from the "big idea" and complete system overhauls to the seemingly small elimination of a single key stroke or saving one penny.

WHY Excellent Organizations Do It Differently

Excellent organizations understand that their options are to constantly improve or to die. They know the feeling of accomplishment and pride that comes with innovating and improving, and they want to feel it again. They understand that one drop of improvement inspires and encourages the next drop and then the next until those drops have carved a Grand Canyon of an organization. They understand that organizations that have truly implemented a "constant improvement" culture can document average annual constant improvement in terms of reduced errors, cost savings, and / or customer satisfaction ratings of five to ten percent per year.

WHERE Is Your Organization Today?

Litmus Test #9 will provide insight regarding where your organization is today on the journey from stuck-in-a-rut toward continual improvement.

LITMUS TEST #9: Processes

Complete here or download your free *Organization Whisperer Toolkit* from our website at www.theorganizationwhisperer.com/kit.

◉ What improvements in operational processes have been implemented in the past six months?

1. _____
2. _____
3. _____
4. _____
5. _____

◉ What has been the measurable, documentable impact of each of these improvements?

1. _____
2. _____
3. _____
4. _____
5. _____

HOW to Become Excellent

Core Action #9 will ripple your organization toward faster, cheaper, constantly improving processes.

CORE ACTION #9

✓ Ask all of Staff to respond to the "Policies and Procedures" worksheet and the "Lean Sources of Waste Checklist" at the end of this chapter.

✓ Ask your Succession Planning Committee to review, cost-benefit, and prioritize the returned recommendations. The committee may wish to use the Core Action #6 "OFI's Planning Kit " for guidance.

✓ Ask invested parties for each of the identified recommendations to lead the implementation of that recommendation. They may wish to use the Core Action #7 "Do It Action / Date Certain" implementation worksheet for guidance.

WHO Will Perform This Action

All staff will innovate. The Succession Team will analyze, synthesize, cost-benefit, and prioritize. Invested parties for each recommendation will lead implementation.

WHEN Will This Action Be Completed?

Excellent organizations operate with a sense of urgency that they are either improving or dying. They are also a family of innovating, constant improvement junkies who always need that next "fix" of accomplishment. All Staff will return their "Policies and Procedures" worksheets and their "Lean Sources of Waste" worksheets by:

Date: _____

Time: _____

The Succession Team will have reviewed, cost-benefitted and prioritized the returned recommendations, using the "OFI's Planning Kit," by:

Date: _____

Time: _____

Invested parties will have completed their "Do It" implementation worksheet by:

Date: _____

Time: _____

The Organization Whisperer Toolkit
Policies and Procedures

The "Policies and Procedures" worksheet Socratically guides you through identifying specific core process steps that can be improved. Complete here or download your free *Organization Whisperer Toolkit* from our website at www.theorganizationwhisperer.com/kit.

WHAT are the functions that you perform most often on a daily basis:
1)
2)
3)
4)
5)
6)
7)
8)
9)

WHAT are the most critical/important functions that you perform (daily, weekly, annually):
1)
2)
3)
4)
5)
6)
7)
8)
9)

WHAT are other functions that you perform that someone else would need to perform in your absence:

1)

2)

3)

4)

5)

For **EACH** function identified above, please provide the following:

WHY is this function performed (Code? State Law? City Ordinance? Customer Service? Audit Best Practices? etc.):

WHEN is it performed (hourly? weekly? Upon request?):

WHO (you and anyone else) performs it:

HOW is the function performed (explain in clear detail each step of how to perform this function so that someone could read your instructions and successfully perform this function):

ADDITIONAL important information about this function:

Key important words / phrases and their meanings:

Relevant forms, their purposes, and how to fill them out (please attach copies):

Relevant computer screens / programs / reports, their purposes, and how to fill them out (please attach copies):

Most common questions / requests, and how to respond:

Important deadlines and why:

Related fees:

Important related laws:

Important Reports (Please Attach Copies), Information on How to Read Them and/or Fill Them Out:

Staff/Departments/Agencies/Vendors Who Contribute to this Function, How They Contribute:

ADDITIONAL important information about this function:

What is the purpose of this function? What is contributed? Who is benefitted by the performance of this function?

Could this function be performed more quickly or efficiently? If so, how?

Is there task duplication that could be eliminated? Explain.

Are there bottlenecks or delays in the process? Explain.

Are there technological inadequacies/obstructions that hamper efficient performance? Explain.

Are there any additional obstructions to the efficient/successful performance of this function (Laws, Rules, Poor Coordination, Poor Human Performance, etc.)? Explain.

What would be an indicator(s) of improved performance in this function (Performed Faster, Cost-savings, Fewer Errors, Shorter Customer Wait Time, etc.)?

How would you adapt/change/innovate/improve this function in order to achieve the desired improvement in the performance Indicator that you have identified?

The Organization Whisperer Toolkit
Lean Sources

This tool informs you about eight most common causes of inefficient processes so that you can be alert for them, and reduce their negative impact, in your organization. Complete here or download your free *Organization Whisperer Toolkit* at www.theorganizationwhisperer.com/kit.

PROCESS:

Identify the following for this process.

DEFECTS • Reworks and incorrect documentation impacting the organization's ability to meet customers' expectations of service and products.

OVER PRODUCTION • Making more than is immediately required.

WAITING • Waiting for parts, information, instructions and equipment due to unbalanced workloads, bottlenecks, poor coordination, etc.

NOT UTILIZING HUMAN TALENT • Un-used abilities, knowledge, skills, creativity, enthusiasm.

TRANSPORTATION • Unnecessary movement /transport of staff, customers, resources, and products.

INVENTORY • Avoidable storing of parts, pieces, documentation, data.

MOTION • Unnecessary bending, turning, reaching, lifting.

EXCESS PROCESSING • Unnecessary or unused rules, regulations, data, reports resulting in increased telephone wait-times, in-line wait times and batch and / or work backlogs.

Core Action #10—Resources

Moving from Too Much or Too Little to Just Right

The most important ability is avail-ability.

REAL LIFE: A company was located on two floors of a building. They had one copy machine, which was placed on the floor that made fifteen percent of the copies.

REAL LIFE: In a college Health and Fitness Bicycling class, the professor kept praising an expensive European racing bike owned by one of the students. At the end of the semester that bike had logged the least miles because it was always broken.

WHAT Excellent Organizations Do Differently

Excellent organizations invest in resources that efficiently, effectively and reliably contribute toward achieving the organization's Mission.

WHY Excellent Organizations Do It Differently

Investing in efficient reliable resources creates procedural reliability, fiscal cost-effectiveness, and subtly contributes to the overall organizational atmosphere of excellence.

WHERE Is Your Organization Today?

Litmus Test #10 will help you determine where your organization is on the continuum between extravagant or inadequate resources to resources that are adequate and reliable.

LITMUS TEST #10: Resources

Complete here or download your free *Organization Whisperer Toolkit* from our website at www.theorganizationwhisperer.com/kit.

⦿ At this moment what are the three most beneficial improvements that could be made in your organization's equipment? Consider, for example, moving specific equipment to a more effective location, replacing pieces of worn-out equipment, or saving rental costs by eliminating unused accessories.

1. _____

2. _____

3. _____

HOW to Become Excellent

Core Action #10 will ripple your organization toward effective, efficient resource management.

CORE ACTION #10

To move toward the desired goal of an organization with "just right" resources, consider the following action for organizational improvement.

   ✓ Use the "Equipment Check-up Checklist" at the end of this chapter to help inventory both existing and needed equipment and determine future needs. Then, act toward implementing those needs.

WHO Will Perform This Action

This Action might be assigned to the person(s) in the organization who has or have the most interest in and / or the most job-related investment in the quality, condition, and reliability of the office's equipment.

The Equipment Team in your organization:

1. _____

2. _____

3. _____

WHEN Will This Action Be Completed?

This action will be completed as soon as possible, hopefully before the next equipment breakdown or the next monthly payment for unused bells and whistles. The Equipment Team will have completed their "Equipment Check-Up Checklist" by:

Date: _____

Time: _____

The Organization Whisperer Toolkit
Equipment Check-up Checklist

This checklist is a planning tool to help you manage your equipment resources and make necessary improvements. Complete here or download your free *Organization Whisperer Toolkit* from our website at www.theorganizationwhisperer.com/kit.

Existing Equipment	Current Capacity	Dependability	Location
List all current equipment	Too Low/Correct/ Not Fully Utilized	Y/N (Explain)	Ideal / Move (Explain)

Equipment Needed	Capacity Needed	Ideal Location
List equipment needed	Slightly more than average projected usage	(Explain)

Core Action #11—Relationships

Moving from Me to Win-Win-Win

An organization can be only as good as its weakest link.

REAL LIFE: A "rock star" CEO was being highly praised for his "brilliant" turn-around of a large but struggling company. Subsequently, he was hired away to perform the same "magic" at a different company where, for the next three years, he failed miserably and was eventually terminated. When asked why he had both succeeded and failed so spectacularly, he replied, "I was the same person executing the same principles; the difference was that the organization, its partners, and vendors supported me in one environment and opposed me in the other. One person cannot create success for an entire organization; organizational success requires the cooperative efforts of the entire extended team."

WHAT Excellent Organizations Do Differently

Mediocre organizations do not think much about how their relationships impact the organization's performance, quality of service, and image. Excellent organizations consider each vendor or partner to be a part of the organization and they monitor the performance and quality of service of their partners/vendors as if they were an internal department of the organization. Excellent organizations also work with only partners and vendors who understand and support a "win-win-win" relationship, in which the partner or vendor buys into and contributes toward achieving the organization's mission, so that the relationship provides a "win" for the organization's mission, the organization, and the partner or vendor.

WHY Excellent Organizations Do It Differently

Excellent organizations know that an organization is only as good as its weakest team member and that partners and vendors are a critical part of "the team".

REAL LIFE: Company A maintained a relationship with a supplier even though that supplier was constantly failing to make delivery deadlines. Ultimately, Company A went bankrupt because it lost most of its customers due to not being able to deliver product.

WHERE Is Your Organization Today?

Litmus Test #11 will provide insight regarding the degree to which your organization has maximized the quality and the potential of its extended relationships.

LITMUS TEST #11: Relationships

Complete here or download your free *Organization Whisperer Toolkit* from our website at www.theorganizationwhisperer.com/kit.

- ◉ Take this "Relationships Litmus Test": List your organization's 5 most critical relationships and rate (from 1 to 10) the degree to which they contribute to, or obstruct, your organization's ability to achieve this mission.

    1)

    2)

    3)

    4)

    5)

What can I do **TODAY** to help DFAS achieve its goals?

Ben, Vendor Pay Technician

HOW to Become Excellent

Core Action #11 will ripple your organization toward triple-win relationships.

CORE ACTION #11

Review the results of your "Relationships Litmus Test," then take the following actions:

- ✓ Complete the "Relationships Required / Desired" worksheet at the end of this chapter to identify relationships that are both required and desired by the organization, both internally, across departments within the organization, and externally, with vendors and partners.

- ✓ Complete the "Relationships Challenges / Recommendations" worksheet at the end of this chapter to identify specific opportunities for improvement (OFI) across all of your most important required and desired relationships.

- ✓ Once the Litmus Test and the two action worksheets have been completed, and the Opportunities for Improvement (OFI's) identified, those OFI's need to be "3-Why'd" (see Core Action #5 and corresponding worksheet) to verify their core challenges and opportunities.

- ✓ All 3-Why'd OFI's need to be synthesized and consolidated to the degree that they can be. They need to be cost-benefitted. Consider the "bang for the buck" delivered with each improvement. Finally, prioritize opportunities into a "most beneficial" desired order of implementation and implement in that order of priority. Use the Action #7 "Do It" worksheet to assist you.

WHO Will Perform This Action

This Action would provide an excellent learning experience for a combination of your Succession Team and additional staff members that may be invested or impacted by some of the partner and vendor relationships.

The Relationships Review Team in your organization:

1. _____
2. _____
3. _____
4. _____
5. _____

WHEN Will this Action be Completed?

The Implementation target dates will be documented in the "WHEN" column of the "Do It" implementation worksheet that you just completed in Core Action #11.

The Organization Whisperer Toolkit
Relationships Required / Desired

This planning worksheet will help you to identify and analyze the relationships that your organization already has and the relationships that it needs to develop. Complete here or download your free *Organization Whisperer Toolkit* at www.theorganizationwhisperer.com/kit.

RELATIONSHIPS (INTERNAL)	RELATIONSHIPS (EXTERNAL)
REQUIRED	REQUIRED
1)	1)
2)	2)
3)	3)
4)	4)
DESIRED	DESIRED
1)	1)
2)	2)
3)	3)
4)	4)

The Organization Whisperer Toolkit
Relationships Challenges and Recommendations

This planning tool will help you to identify challenges that currently exist in your organizational relationships and make key recommendations for improvement. Complete here or download your free *Organization Whisperer Toolkit* from our website at www.theorganizationwhisperer.com/kit.

CHALLENGES	RECOMMENDATIONS
DELAYS 1) 2)	DELAYS 1) 2)
DUPLICATIONS 1) 2)	DUPLICATIONS 1) 2)
PASS THE BUCKS 1) 2)	PASS THE BUCKS 1) 2)
MISCONNECTS 1) 2)	MISCONNECTS 1) 2)

BOTTLE-NECKS	BOTTLE-NECKS
1)	1)
2)	2)
HUMAN CHALLENGES	HUMAN CHALLENGES
1)	1)
2)	2)
HUMAN HEROES	HUMAN HEROES
1)	1)
2)	2)
OPPORTUNITIES	OPPORTUNITIES
1)	1)
2)	2)

Core Action #12—Habit

Moving from "Repeat What?" to Excellence as a Habit

Attitudes and actions combine to create self-fulfilling cycles.

People and organizations that operate on the basis of negative expectations and narcissistic actions encourage responses of resentment and resistance, which creates a downward spiral of failure. Constructive inclusion encourages positive, cooperative responses which build teamwork that produces an upward spiral of success.

Excellence is not achieved with one isolated action; it is achieved through constantly repeating specific actions that are known to ripple, to spiral success.

FABLE: Two piggies were walking through the woods when, suddenly, a wolf came charging after them. The piggies ran. One of the piggies, the one who consistently worked out three days a week, got away. The other piggy got eaten.

REAL LIFE: For years Southwest Airlines had been a "poster child" for having a "positive performance management culture." One month after the events of September 11th, 2001, at the nadir of the airline industry, financial analysts estimated that Southwest Airlines alone represented 90 percent of the total net value of the American airline industry, verifying that, when the wolf came calling, Southwest Airlines had consistently implemented their belief in and commitment to a positive performance culture to build a very sound "house of bricks."

WHAT Excellent Organizations Do Differently

Excellent organizations constantly strengthen the bonds within their positive-focused family. In addition, they constantly improve the efficiency and effectiveness of their processes by repeating and maximizing the potential benefits of the specific core actions of excellence shared in this book.

WHY Excellent Organizations Do It Differently

The Twelve Core Actions work. Remember the Gallup study that found that organizations that build and sustain a positive family culture and constantly improve their processes build an organizational house of bricks that produces:

- 19 percent improved staff stability
- 22.5 percent improved productivity
- 48 percent improved profitability
- 5-7 percent sustained annual improvement

WHERE Is Your Organization Today?

In Litmus Test #12 you will once again take the Organization Whisperer Diagnostic to determine how much progress your organization has made since you last took the Diagnostic.

LITMUS TEST # 12: Habit

Complete here or download your free *Organization Whisperer Toolkit* from our website at www.theorganizationwhisperer.com/kit.

◉ Along with as many managers and staff as you would like to include, take the "Organization Whisperer Leadership Diagnostic" again.

◉ Compare these latest diagnostic scores to the scores that you reported in the initial baseline diagnostic that you took at the beginning of the book. So, how are you doing? How much has your organization improved? Has the implementation of some of the Core Actions been beneficial? Where are the opportunities for continued improvements? Record your insights:

◉ NOTE: Keep a dated record of both diagnostic sets of scores so that you can maintain an ongoing history of your organization's progress. Be aware that many Organization Whisperers find that their Diagnostic scores actually decline in cycles 3 and 4, not because their organization is deteriorating, but because the Whisperer and the Organization have developed more understanding and confidence and, consequently, have elevated their expectations and begin scoring themselves more critically based upon higher expectations.

HOW to Become Excellent

Core Action #12 will direct you in creating constant ripples of excellence that will sustain an on-going spiral of success.

CORE ACTION #12

Complete here or download your free *Organization Whisperer Toolkit* from our website at www.theorganizationwhisperer.com/kit.

✓ Go back to Core Action #1. Retake all twelve Litmus Tests in chapters one through twelve. Perform the corresponding twelve Core Actions a second time. It will be a lot easier this time, and even easier the third time. Soon, it will become a habit.

✓ Repeat… and Repeat… and…

WHO Will Perform This Action

You, your Succession Team, your organizational cheerleaders, staff who are experts or invested parties in a particular project, and anyone else who wishes to volunteer to help improve the organization will all be a part of this   journey. An organization can be only as strong as the combined contributions to its success.

WHEN Will this Action be Completed?

Immediately and constantly. You will constantly monitor and measure your performance, and will constantly implement actions to improve as long as your organization strives to stay one step ahead of the wolf, as long as it desires to survive and prosper, and as long as your team enjoys the challenge of pursuing those elusive adrenalin rushes of joy that occur when, due to constant effort, cooperation, and commitment, everything clicks and excellence is achieved.

Final Notes

It is not the critic who counts;
Not the person who points out how the strong person stumbled
Or where the doer of deeds could have done them better.

The credit belongs to the person who is actually in the arena,
Whose face is marred by dust and sweat and blood;
Who strives valiantly;

Who errs and comes short again and again;
Who knows great enthusiasms,
The great devotions;

Who spends their self in a worthy cause;
Who at the best, know in the end the triumph of high achievement,
And who, at the worst, if they fail, at least fails while daring greatly;

So that their place shall never be with those timid souls
who neither knew victory nor defeat.

Theodore Roosevelt

Fail to honor people, and they will not honor you.
But of the good Leaders, who talk little,
When the work is done and the goals achieved,
Their people will say, "We did this ourselves."

Lao Tse

This book is meant to be a "Starter Kit" that explains how excellent organizations think, and describes a few specific core actions that separate them from the pack. Once this book has given you the initial insight and kick start, once you "get it", you are encouraged to not limit yourself to the few starter actions provided here, but rather to innovate and expand as far as the creativity of your purpose-focused family can imagine.

Organization Whisperers have the knowledge and the tools to dramatically improve organizations and individual lives. By doing so and seeing the positive impacts that they have created, the Organization Whisperer's own life is constantly deeply enriched. There cannot be any more powerful reason to start today.

> **REAL LIFE:** A little boy tossed a small rock high into the sky, watched it drop into the water, and then watched the ripples that the small rock had created spread out, influencing a wide area of the lake's placid surface. Eventually, the ripples faded away. The boy picked up another rock.

www.ingramcontent.com/pod-product-compliance
Lightning Source LLC
Chambersburg PA
CBHW051220200326
41519CB00025B/7188